PEN

EVERYBO

C000152490

Brian Cathcart has been a journalist for more than thirty years, working for Reuters, the *Independent*, the *Independent on Sunday* (where he was deputy editor) and the *New Statesman* (assistant editor and media columnist). He is the author of several books, including *Were You Still Up for Portillo?* and the award-winning *The Case of Stephen Lawrence*. As a journalist he has campaigned for justice for Barry George, who was wrongly convicted of killing Jill Dando, and for the families of the young soldiers killed at Deepcut army barracks. In 2008–10 he was specialist adviser to the Commons media select committee and he has since written about the hacking crisis and media reform for Index on Censorship, Hacked Off, the *Guardian*, the *Financial Times*, the *Independent*, the *Daily Beast*, CNN, Inforrm and others. He has been professor of journalism at Kingston University London since 2005.

Additional research for this book has been conducted by Natalie Peck, Christopher Ford and Dulcie Lee.

Everybody's Hacked Off

Why we don't have the press we deserve and what to do about it

BRIAN CATHCART

with an Introduction by Hugh Grant

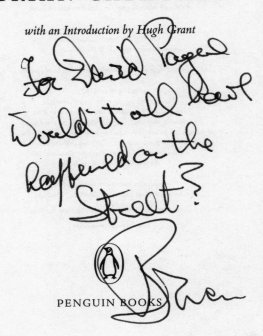

PENGUIN BOOKS

PENGUIN BOOKS

Published by the Penguin Group
Penguin Books Ltd, 80 Strand, London WC2R ORL, England
Penguin Group (USA) Inc., 375 Hudson Street, New York, New York 10014, USA
Penguin Group (Canada), 90 Eglinton Avenue East, Suite 700, Toronto, Ontario, Canada M4P 2Y3
(a division of Pearson Penguin Canada Inc.)
Penguin Ireland, 25 St Stephen's Green, Dublin 2, Ireland
(a division of Penguin Books Ltd)
Penguin Group (Australia), 707 Collins Street, Melbourne, Victoria 3008, Australia
(a division of Pearson Australia Group Pty Ltd)
Penguin Books India Pvt Ltd, 11 Community Centre, Panchsheel Park, New Delhi – 110 017, India
Penguin Group (NZ), 67 Apollo Drive, Rosedale, Auckland 0632, New Zealand
(a division of Pearson New Zealand Ltd)
Penguin Books (South Africa) (Pty) Ltd, Block D, Rosebank Office Park, 181 Jan Smuts Avenue,
Parktown North, Gauteng 2193, South Africa

Penguin Books Ltd, Registered Offices: 80 Strand, London WC2R ORL, England

www.penguin.com

First published 2012
Published simultaneously as a Penguin Special ebook
001

Copyright © Brian Cathcart, 2012
Introduction copyright © Hugh Grant, 2012

The moral right of the copyright holders has been asserted

Typeset by Firstsource Solutions Ltd
Printed in Great Britain by Clays Ltd, St Ives plc

A CIP catalogue record for this book is available from the British Library

ISBN: 978-0-241-96556-6

Contents

Contents

Introduction

As I write this, it is twelve months since the beginning of the Leveson Inquiry and fourteen months since the Milly Dowler revelations, and there are some who say it's all old news, overkill, has taken too long, cost too much, lost its direction, lost its momentum. I don't agree. I think this is where it gets really interesting. I think we are at last approaching a defining moment – defining for the British press, of course, but also defining in terms of individuals. In the next six months we will learn who a lot of people really are.

I imagine that when this short book is published Lord Justice Leveson will still be writing his report. We don't know what he will say, but we do know what he has heard over the past twelve months. He's heard about a night-marish pattern of mistreatment of innocent people, of the cynical covering up of wrongdoing, of the industrial-scale quarrying of personal information from confidential data-bases, of the corruption of public officials and the intimidation of politicians – all of it in pursuit, not of news that might serve the public interest, but of corporate profit. And he heard how at least four of our last five governments have not only done nothing about any of these things, but have bent over backwards to oblige the corporations and individual owners of those papers that were most guilty.

Let us say that, on the basis of this evidence, Leveson recommends that the press should no longer be the only industry in this country with the power to damage citizens' lives that is regulated solely by itself. Let's say he recommends that the Press Complaints Commission must go, replaced not by the industry's suggested son-of-PCC (rejected by all victims), but by a proper regulator that is independent of the industry and of government. One that has a new and beefed-up code of practice and, for the first time, real teeth to sanction transgressions of that code. What will happen then?

It will be war. And here's how the battlefield will look.

In the middle will be the prize: the politicians with the power to either enact Leveson's recommendations or kick them into the long grass. Last July, after the Dowler revelations, these politicians all talked a good game, but last June, pre-Dowler, a lot of them were sipping champagne on Rupert Murdoch's lawn. There are notable and noble exceptions, but a great many of them, when the crunch comes, could go either way.

Fighting for their votes on one side will be the tabloid press (backed by *The Times* and the *Telegraph*), doing everything in its power to prevent itself being decently regulated, to preserve its lucrative business model, to prolong a three-decade honeymoon of relative immunity from the law, to preserve its power to appropriate the rights of citizens for corporate gain, to effectively tell elected politicians how they want the country run.

Their power is daunting. They have the front pages, editorials and opinion pieces, the hatchet jobs and the editorialized news reporting. They have people of influence who owe them favours or are paid by them, or might in the future (if they toe the line) be paid by them. They also have people of influence who fear them, who fear their vengeance in terms of exposure of personal lives or loss of electoral support. They have huge sums of money (for all the talk about papers dying, the major tabloids still turn healthy profits) to spend on the best lawyers, lobbyists, dirt-diggers, private investigators. They have a power so great that few in recent British history have been able to withstand it.

On the other side you have the few voices in parliament who have spoken out all along against press abuses, such as Tom Watson, Chris Bryant and Lord Fowler. You have the lawyers who pioneered the first civil cases on hacking (and who were duly hacked and put under surveillance for their troubles). You have the *Guardian* and, on the whole, the *Independent*, with their modest circulations. And you have a few small campaign groups, of which one is Hacked Off.

Hacked Off is an unlikely bunch. For the past year it has had at its core three balanced and principled academics, a few clever lawyers, one passionate, hyperactive ex-LibDem MP, two horrified journalists, one cross film actor and one livid comedian. It campaigned for a full public inquiry into phone hacking and thanks to the help and bravery of the Dowler family it managed to get one. It also helped write the terms of reference.

It raises its hand when current affairs broadcasters are looking for someone to debate with a tabloid editor or apologist. (The system is that the broadcaster – *Newsnight*, *Today*, whatever – then refuses to book the academics or the ex-MP who are most expert and eloquent, and insist instead on the actor or comedian because they are better for the ratings. Then they like to demand of the actor and comedian, on air, 'Why should anyone listen to you?' Or 'Isn't this all just about celebrities?')

Everyone (except our lone employee) has had other jobs to do. Corners of pubs and coffee shops were our meeting rooms. Some finance has come from charitable trusts and some from individual donations, large and small. As I write we are trying to morph into something more professional to meet the huge challenge ahead. Donations would be very welcome.

I believe that Lord Justice Leveson will recommend a new regulator and that the battle that follows will be massively uneven. This is why it will be as much a defining moment for individuals such as you, reading this, now, as it is for the future of the press. We think that while the press should and must be always be, in the best British tradition, free, spiky, nosey, irreverent, sceptical and never fawning to power or success, it should no longer be, in a very unBritish way, cowardly, manipulative, greedy, bullying, immune to law and intoxicated with its own power. No one wants a state-run media, but what we have had for thirty-odd years is media-run state. If you agree with that and you stand up and say so over the coming months you may make yourself a target. But if you agree with it and say nothing, or, worse, you disguise your fear of saying something with pious and convenient posturing about free speech as though you owned the concept (I believe the verb is 'to gove'), you will be safe. And if you do that, nothing will change. So it's a defining moment, for all of us.

Please define yourself on our side. This book sets out the case for change, but just reading it is not enough. At the end you will find suggestions for small things you can do to help make change happen and to show the world that, like me and like the others in this campaign, you also are hacked off.

Finally, four key facts about Brian Cathcart, the author of this book:

1. He was one of the two founders of Hacked Off.
2. Unlike some of us, his motives can never (albeit unfairly) be ascribed to any personal grudge or run-in with the press. They are purely to do with outrage at what happened to the profession he loves, believes in, teaches and has excelled at.
3. He fools many with his air of the mild-mannered academic. Don't be fooled.
4. His book (this book) says everything I have said above, but much, much better. Everyone should read it.

Hugh Grant
August 2012

This Time is Different

Over the course of his inquiry into the culture, practices and ethics of the press, Lord Justice Leveson often interrupted the formal questioning to discuss points with witnesses, and on those occasions he would sometimes share his thoughts and concerns in a surprisingly candid fashion. Everybody knew he could be sharp-tongued but in these moments he was at his most amiable, very much the honest seeker after truth. Occasionally he would make short speeches, unburdening himself of whatever concern was weighing upon him, and when he did this in the later hearings it was often to express a fear. He was worried, he would say, that the report he was due to write about his eight-month, £5-million public investigation would end up as nothing more than another volume on the bookshelves of journalism academics. He didn't want that to happen. After hearing so many witnesses and working his way through a mountain of written evidence and submissions, he wanted to make a difference, and a lasting one.

It was a natural feeling for someone in his position. Anyone chairing an inquiry would presumably feel the same. And yet for Leveson the fear that all of his efforts would go to waste was especially pressing, because he knew the history. He was not the first eminent person in recent decades to go down this road of examining the conduct of journalists, editors and newspaper proprietors; indeed he was not even the second or third, but more like the seventh or eighth. Since the 1940s there have been three full-blown royal commissions on the press and three other official inquiries and reviews, not to mention other less formal scrutinies. Most of them took evidence, as Leveson did, from mighty newspaper proprietors and their editors, and every one of them produced a report. And in all of those cases, as Leveson knew, the effort was largely wasted. The careful analysis of the evidence, the judicious allocation of responsibility, the thoughtful and usually rather timid proposals – they were published, discussed in a cursory or dismissive way, and then simply placed on the shelf. At best their lists of recommendations were paid a little tardy lip service. So it may well be true that the only people with working knowledge of those reports today are the academics who are paid to study the forgotten and obscure.

If all precedent suggests that press inquiries are a waste of time it is no wonder Leveson was worried. Why would he, or anyone else, assume that the report of 2012 would have a different fate from that of 1993, or 1990, or 1977, or 1969, or 1962, or 1949? After all, the forces that consigned all those reports to the shelf of academic obscurity still exist and are still powerful – and they are determined to secure the same outcome again.

On all of those past occasions it was the proprietors and editors of the national newspapers who blocked change, sidestepping or frustrating every effort to make them more accountable to the public. Their tactics tended to follow a pattern. When the inquiries were established the owners and editors complained of a fix or a government overreaction. Where they gave evidence it was usually grudging and defensive, insisting that no change was necessary, or alternatively that if something needed to be done they were the only people who could possibly know what it was and how to do it. In every case the inquiry report declared that those who ran the press had to change their ways, and specific measures were proposed. And in every case the editors and owners failed, or rather refused, to oblige. Sometimes they would indignantly reject a proposal as an outrage against press freedom; sometimes they would drag their feet for years before making the smallest possible concession; and sometimes they could engage in plain deception, doing something subtly but significantly different from what had been asked.

It was relatively easy for them because they had great power. For one thing, they could decide what was reported about these inquiries and what was not; which opinions reached a wide audience and which did not. For another, like the guest at a dinner party who speaks only through a megaphone, they were almost impossible to argue with: they simply out-shouted their critics. This made them more or less immune to public pressure. Meanwhile they wielded a different kind of power over the politicians, who had to decide whether official reports were implemented, or watered down, or kicked into the infamous long grass. Again and again governments ducked confrontation, either because they wished to curry favour with newspapers that could influence voters, or because they feared the consequences of upsetting them. It is a nice irony that several of these inquiries, just like Leveson, were explicitly tasked with examining the issue of press power, and then themselves became victims of that same power.

Time, too, was always on the side of the papers. It invariably required a long accumulation of problems with the press – a head of steam – to provoke an inquiry. Then the inquiry itself took months or even years, in which time the steam pressure would inevitably fall and the original problems would begin to feel remote to the public. The report had to be written, published and discussed, and then the newspapers and the government of the day had to give their reactions, all of which took more time. And always the next election was drawing nearer, and the need steadily grew for politicians to keep their friends, or at least avoid making enemies, in the press.

This is not just history. It could happen again. Indeed the editors and proprietors of most of today's national newspapers are determined that it *will* happen again, and they are using all their old tricks and some new ones to ensure that it does. They laid low during the worst of the Leveson storm but even before the hearings ended they began turning up the megaphone, blaring out their messages. Free speech is in danger, they say. Why should the whole of the press suffer because of the actions of one rogue company, they ask. Precious jobs in journalism may be lost, they warn. MPs and celebrities are taking revenge for having their misdeeds exposed ... Meanwhile they publish with extravagant prominence every hostile titbit they can find about their more prominent critics: Steve Coogan, J. K. Rowling, Charlotte Church, Hugh Grant, Tom Watson MP ... They want the public to hate or resent these people. Leveson himself, and his inquiry team, are also targets, with papers attacking his conduct of the inquiry and finding fault with his selection of advisers.

As for the politicians, when the inquiry was set up in July 2011 there was cross-party consensus that the time had come for a historic change. Many confessed that they had been weak in failing to stand up to the press; some spoke of decades of fear while others recalled with embarrassment the parties, lunches, tickets for big events and other treats that had been used to seduce them. They seemed genuinely excited at the thought of getting the press beast off their backs. But time, that old ally of editors and proprietors, is again doing its work. Every day and every week brings the next general election closer, and every day and every week pushes the shocked emotions of 2011 and the memory of the Dowlers and the McCanns farther into the past. So now again the siren voices are calling to the politicians to take the easy way out, to give the papers one more chance to put their own house in order, to shelve the Leveson report. No wonder the judge was worried.

And he had only to look at recent experience in Australia to become more so. There, a senior judge, Ray Finkelstein, published a report on media conduct and regulation in March 2012, only to see it buried beneath a heap of press abuse and condemnation. The academic and journalist Matthew Ricketson, who advised the inquiry, has described how, in his view, the Australian papers grossly under-reported the evidence given to the inquiry (which included 762 submissions expressing dissatisfaction with the news media and just four expressing satisfaction) and then equally grossly misreported the findings. 'Anyone who relied on the mainstream news media for their knowledge of the media inquiry's report could be forgiven for thinking that we had recommended the federal government ... stuff freedom of the press into a sack and dump it out at sea,' he wrote. One editor described the report as 'the most outrageous assault on our democracy in the history of the media' and suggested it would usher in conditions reminiscent of Stalin's Soviet Union or North Korea.[1]

But we should not despair. There are some good reasons to hope that what happened to the previous British reports may not happen again, because this time is certainly different. It is different mainly because, though the editors and proprietors may still be powerful, they do not control the news agenda to the degree that they once did. Look, for example, at one small aspect of what happened in July 2011. It was on the afternoon of Monday 4 July that the *Guardian* revealed online that the *News of the World* had hacked the phone of murdered teenager Milly Dowler. There was instant and widespread horror and the story was soon dominating the television and radio bulletins. That evening, however, the editors of most of the national daily newspapers made a striking choice. Usually they will embrace any story that is firing up the emotions of their readers, but not this time. The *Sun*, the *Daily Mirror*, the *Daily Star* and the *Daily Express* all judged that this outrage against a dead child and her bereaved family did not even merit a paragraph on the front page. The *Daily Mail* and *The Times*, meanwhile, pushed the story down to second or third billing, the *Mail* placing its report in the shadow of a much bigger headline about tax and the elderly. Dowler may have been the lead story for the *Daily Telegraph*, the *Independent* and, naturally, the *Guardian*, but significantly those three account for less than one eighth of daily newspaper readership.

It was only the latest though perhaps the most shameless act in a sustained effort to suppress the story of hacking, to hide it from the readers; and as recently as ten years ago it might have succeeded. This time it didn't. Thanks to broadcast news and the internet, newspaper editors were unable to divert or to smother the fury that would lead within a couple of weeks to the closure of the *News of the World*, the abandonment of Rupert Murdoch's bid for outright ownership of BSkyB and the establishment of the Leveson Inquiry. It was a sign that while newspapers may still influence the daily news agenda they can no longer steer it as they once did. And this change also affected the way we all experienced the Leveson Inquiry once it started work. Where all previous inquiries into the press over the past sixty years were reported, explained and interpreted principally by the very press that was being scrutinized, Leveson ensured that his inquiry took place live online before a large audience, and it was also reported much more extensively in broadcast news than its predecessors. The editors could warp and twist the proceedings in their own pages – and they did their worst – but they could not conceal the fact that they were on trial.

And not only did Leveson go out to the world but the world also came to Leveson, in an unprecedented manner. Legions of people with stories of press abuse signed up as 'core participant victims', or sent in submissions, or lent their experiences to omnibus collections of stories. MPs and celebrities, academics and victims of crime, lawyers and ordinary people caught in the media crossfire: they all testified. And a great variety of organizations gave evidence too. Where in 1947–9 or in 1962 or in 1990 the inquiries had been largely dialogues between politicians and senior journalists or their employers, with a few others on the fringe, in 2011–12 at the Leveson Inquiry civil society moved in. The British Psychological Society had something to contribute, as did the Federation of Poles in Great Britain, as did the Hillsborough Family Support Group, the National AIDS Trust and the College of Social Work, and many others too. This was no longer just the establishment talking to the establishment; the public was involved.

Another story. *The Times* regularly carries opinion polls, which are conducted for it by the Populus organization. In June 2012 the paper asked Populus to seek the views of the public about the Leveson Inquiry, and so respondents were asked whether they agreed or disagreed with the proposition that 'the Leveson Inquiry will lead to more effective regulation of the press, offering better protection to members of the public against unwarranted intrusion into their private lives'. Fifty-nine per cent said they agreed, while 27 per cent disagreed. How did *The Times* report this finding? It didn't. Its report went like this:

> ... a new Populus poll for *The Times* suggests that the public believe the hearings have lost their way. The poll found 61 per cent agreeing that the 'Leveson inquiry has lost its way as a procession of politicians, journalists and celebrities have simply tried to defend themselves against one another's allegations'. The same proportion felt that it has 'received too much coverage in the media' given the other news around. Less than half, 44 per cent, thought the inquiry 'will result in a healthier, more arms-length relationship between politicians and the media'.

So while the poll showed that a comfortable majority trusted Leveson to do a good job, the newspaper somehow did not find room for this fact. Instead it reported responses to two rather loaded questions, which appeared to show Leveson in a negative light. And it said that 'only' 44 per cent felt the inquiry would improve relations between politicians and the press without mentioning that even fewer, 36 per cent, took the opposite view. (In other words, more people trusted Leveson on this than not.) You could hardly find a more vivid example of corporate denial. But more important than the *Times*'s denial was the public's faith. Despite months of negative reporting and distortion in most of the national press, people backed the Leveson process. The drip-drip of complaints by newspaper columnists that Leveson was boring, out of touch, dictatorial, running beyond his remit, killing press freedom, in thrall to celebrities and unfair to editors failed to produce the desired effect. And this was not a freak finding: other polls and studies around that time, notably one by the Institute for Public Policy Research, confirmed that the public strongly favoured change.[2]

But the weeks and months have been slipping by and time is on the side of the editors and proprietors. Their drip-drip of propaganda, meanwhile, has become a steady flow. They intend to drown the argument.

They have another problem, though, which is that their case is extraordinarily weak. They have a handful of standard arguments that are more or less the ones they and their predecessors have been deploying for decades, but this time, one way or another, the readers, the victims and the critics are able to answer back, exposing the feebleness of the arguments as never before, and showing how isolated are the remaining believers. Few outside the press industry, indeed few outside the upper reaches of that industry, have endorsed the editors' stance. There is a widespread refusal, in particular, to accept their assertion that effective regulation of the press inevitably means the end for freedom of expression – an assertion that has been especially hard to swallow because it comes from a group of people who have so conspicuously betrayed freedom of expression. In an industry which boasts that free expression is guaranteed by the diversity of views it delivers, there was a conspiracy, albeit probably an unspoken one, to deny readers news not only about the wrongdoings of journalists, but also about a cynical cover-up by the country's biggest media corporation. Month after month the story was buried or ignored, and worse, those who did report it – notably the *Guardian* – were attacked, mocked and belittled for doing so. The people who operated this code of *omerta* make poor champions of free expression.

Worse still, their past evasions and deceptions have caught up with them. The analogy of the Last Chance Saloon may be a weary one, but it still expresses with some potency exactly where they are, and the more so precisely because it is so weary. It was in 1989 that the Tory minister David Mellor told the press it was 'drinking in the Last Chance Saloon'. Last chances are supposed to be finite but Mellor's warning resulted in no real change, so the editors and proprietors have been able to enjoy the hospitality of the saloon for a couple of decades. The time has come to move on.

So is it all over? Are our national newspapers finally going to be made accountable, or are we going to see the same old tricks produce the same result – another decade or two of the Last Chance Saloon, with unaccountable papers bullying and intruding upon innocent people? It is finely balanced. There is a lot of public anger and determination — you might say that everybody's hacked off. But don't forget the power of time; don't underestimate the volume and persistence of the press megaphone; and don't forget that fatal weakness of politicians. (If, for example, action on media reform were to be delayed until 2014, the next election would then be just a year away.) So if we want to be sure of change we must all be ready to make a stand, to insist that this time we see the press made accountable to the public it is supposed to serve. We must demand that government and opposition stand up to the proprietors and editors and their allies. We must oppose further delays, reviews and consultations. We must say: no fixes or fudges, and no more last chances!

We can resist the effects of time by keeping fresh in our minds the reasons why the inquiry was necessary and what it showed us. And we should see the tactics and the arguments of the editors and proprietors for what they are. This short book aims to help.

(When you read the words 'press' and 'newspapers' in this book they usually do not refer to print editions alone. All of our national newspapers run websites, some of them very successful, and the journalism published on these is included. Equally, in this book the two words usually refer to national newspapers and not regional and local ones.)

The Mess We're In

Many of us like sausages and we eat them often, but few of us really want to know very much about how sausages are made, what goes into them and what conditions are like in abattoirs. So it is when we read our daily newspapers: we are often entertained by scandal and sensation stories and we enjoy sharing them with others – gossiping is an almost instinctive activity in human beings – but we rarely stop to consider what goes into those stories, how they are found and made. In general we would probably rather not know. What the phone-hacking scandal did, in a way that had rarely happened before, was to reveal to us some of the inner workings of one news factory, the *News of the World*, and what we saw was revolting.

The basics of the story are straightforward. Between 2000 and 2006 a number of *News of the World* journalists worked with private investigator Glenn Mulcaire (then on a £102,000-a-year exclusive contract with the paper) to access and listen to the private mobile phone voicemail messages of people that interested them. Police believe that 1,081 people were likely to have been victims of this, although the number of potential victims – people for whom Mulcaire had a phone number, making hacking or other illegal information-gathering possible – stretches to 4,775. We will never know the exact total. The targets included celebrities, police officers, victims of crime, royal princes, people in witness protection, cabinet ministers, solicitors, campaigners, journalists and many more. There were also many collateral or secondary victims – ordinary members of the public who for whatever reason were in contact with people of interest to the *News of the World*, or who in some unlucky way strayed into the paper's gun-sights. They include the mothers, fathers, brothers, sisters, friends and associates of people in the news, and even, sometimes, people who happened to have the same or similar names to *News of the World* targets.

It is easy to forget, but this happened before text messages became commonplace and before we had mobile access to email. People used voicemail far more than they would now, meaning that the hackers were accessing a very important channel of private communication. And it was as easy as it was revealing, because the personal security of the targets tended to be weak – people were not alert to the risk – and so was the general security of the mobile phone system. The difficult bit for the hacker was to get hold of the phone numbers in the first place, and also, if necessary, to the PINs and passwords (though many users simply left their phones on factory settings that were known to Mulcaire). After that it was just a matter of dialling in, and, unless the hackers were care-less, the eavesdropping was unlikely to be detected. With so much to gain and so little to stop them, they helped themselves – again and again and again. In one operation against officials in the royal household two hackers phoned three personal mobile numbers more than 600 times to access the mailboxes. This bald explanation, however, does not do justice to the sheer industrial nasti-ness of what happened, so here are a few examples from the many.

Milly Dowler

The most notorious case is also a very revealing one. Amanda 'Milly' Dowler, aged thirteen, disappeared on the evening of 21 March 2002. Shortly before 13 April, with the police hunt at its height, the *News of the World* hacked her mobile phone. She had by then been murdered. Reporters listened to at least four voicemail messages, one of which they transcribed as follows [the redactions are by Surrey Police]: 'Hello Mandy. This is [REDACTED] from [REDACTED] Recruitment Agency. We are ringing because we have interviews starting today at [REDACTED]. Call back on [REDACTED]. Thanks, bye bye.'[3] The paper took this to mean that Milly was alive and, using the name 'Mandy', seeking work in the Midlands, where the agency was based. It sent reporters to the agency to question staff, telling them, according to the Surrey Police account, that they (the reporters) were working 'in full cooperation' with the police. The agency staff then called Surrey Police to check this and the police in turn called the *News of the World* to find out what was going on. The paper stated bluntly that it had acquired its information from Milly's phone and gave detectives its transcript of the message. And despite appeals from the police – and warnings that the message might well have been the work of a hoaxer – the paper reported its supposed angle on the Dowler story in that weekend's edition.

Days later the paper was in touch with Surrey Police again, now telling them it was convinced Milly was looking for factory work in the north of England, and indeed the *News of the World* actually staked out one factory. By now detectives had themselves accessed Milly's voicemails (legally) and they formed the view that the message was intended for someone called 'Nana' rather than 'Mandy'.

Inquiries established that the recruitment agency had a client called Nana, that Milly Dowler's number had by pure chance been entered in their records in mistake for the correct number, and that therefore the message on Milly's phone had been meant for someone else. Informed of all this, the *News of the World* refused to believe it.

Sienna Miller

The actress Sienna Miller was the target of an intensive hacking campaign in 2005–6. Not only were her own communications accessed, but so were those of a network of friends, relatives and associates. When she became suspicious and changed her phone the paper was able to hack the new phone almost immediately. When she changed phones again, this time to one registered with her publicist, again it was hacked straight away. The paper created what Miller called a 'web of surveillance', and police later found the following in Mulcaire's notebooks:

- the number, account number, PIN and password for all three mobile phones used by Miller in this period;
- the mobile phone number, PIN and password of a close friend of hers;
- the mobile phone numbers of her former partner Jude Law;
- the mobile phone numbers of Law's personal assistant;
- the numbers of three different mobile phones used by Miller's publicist;
- the address and home telephone number of Miller's mother.

In addition, the paper had hacked the mobile phone of Miller's stepmother, the designer Kelly Hoppen.

All of this helped the *News of the World* to publish regular stories about Miller and in particular about her relationship with Law. Some of these revealed intimate information such as discussions about the possibility of their having children or becoming engaged, about other relationships, about holiday travel plans and about arguments. While this went on, Miller also found that wherever she went, even to places where she assumed she would have privacy, journalists and photographers would usually be waiting for her. And she may even have compounded the problem because as she grew more suspicious she became reluctant to talk on the phone, which meant callers were more likely to leave messages. Miller told the Leveson Inquiry: 'I was torn between feeling completely paranoid that either someone close to me (a trusted family member or friend) was selling this information to the media or that someone was somehow hacking my telephone ... I remember one occasion where I sat my family and friends down in a room and I accused them of leaking stories to the press as a story had come out that only they had known about. Looking back, it makes me extremely angry that I was forced into being so suspicious of people that I love and care for, and that I had to suffer such feelings of betrayal, especially by those who had done nothing wrong.'

HJK

HJK is an ordinary member of the public who dated a celebrity for a few weeks in 2006. (Whether this is a man or a woman has not been revealed. For convenience HJK is referred to here as a male.) He later learned that Mulcaire had:

- his address, mobile and work phone numbers, PINs and passwords;
- transcripts of voicemail messages between him and the celebrity;
- a record of text and call traffic between them;
- other private information about him and about the celebrity.

As a result of this hacking a journalist turned up on his doorstep and asserted, wrongly, that the celebrity was living with him. HJK sent the reporter away and informed the celebrity, who, fearing that HJK was part of a kiss-and-tell sting, immediately ended their relationship. The journalist then called on HJK again, offered money for an interview and was turned away. When HJK was tipped off that a hostile story about him would be published anyway he warned his employer, who was unsympathetic, apparently fearing his business would be linked to a tabloid scandal. Things deteriorated further when HJK missed important business voicemails left on his phone – they had been accessed by hackers before he was aware of them, and were listed in his phone as already read. He was now blamed and bullied at work, while in the street he was stalked by reporters or photographers. He lived in fear that something malicious about him was about to be published, and saw this as a tactic to make him crack and tell or sell his story. This went on for nine months, ending only after the first hacking arrests in 2006. HJK told the Leveson Inquiry: 'I witnessed my life going up in flames around me.'

Gordon Taylor

As head of the Professional Footballers' Association, Taylor is an influential figure in football, though hardly a household name. Mulcaire, having secured a special bonus contract for the project from the *News of the World*, mounted a hacking operation against Taylor and two of his associates, including Jo Armstrong, his legal adviser. In June 2005 a *News of the World* reporter transcribed thirty-five of these intercepted and recorded voicemails, including one from Armstrong to Taylor that was construed by the paper as evidence they were having an affair. They were not: according to Taylor's solicitor it was actually a message from Armstrong thanking Taylor for things he had said at her father's funeral. On the basis of this false lead, however, a front-page story was drafted, the pair were secretly photographed together and, on the day before publication was due, the paper's chief reporter was sent from London to the Manchester area to confront one of them. It took an adamant and forceful denial and the threat of legal action to prevent publication of the false story.

There was much more to hacking, therefore, than merely eavesdropping on the conversations of celebrities to pick up titbits of gossip. It was a sustained intelligence-gathering operation and it gave the *News of the World* power over people. Reporters might pick up knowledge that could be published or that would need further work in the form of doorstepping and stalking operations. Or they might learn private information that could be used as leverage to persuade sources to cooperate. And this was a very big business at the paper. It has been estimated that *News of the*

World reporters made on average of 4,500 hacking calls per year, and that does not include the calls made by Mulcaire himself, the fixer at the heart of it all. This industrial-scale privacy invasion created an army of victims, in all walks of life. For some the experience was terrifying and generated a wholly unjustified distrust of those closest to them. For others – and many of them only learned years afterwards that it had happened – there is the horror of knowing that *News of the World* reporters knew *and still know* some of their most intimate secrets, and may well have shared them with others.

As News International has acknowledged in a long and continuing series of costly legal settlements with victims, what the hackers were doing was a violation of the human right to privacy. It also broke or was likely to have broken several criminal laws, including the Misuse of Computers Act (1990) and the Regulation of Investigatory Powers Act (2000). The acquisition of the confidential phone numbers may also have breached the Data Protection Act (1998) and in some cases the Fraud Act (2006). And hacking breached at least two clauses of the Press Complaints Commission Editors' Code of Conduct – those relating to privacy and to the use of subterfuge. Other clauses of the code were breached in individual cases, notably those concerned with intrusion into grief or shock, with the protection of children and with the protection of victims of sexual assault. It is just about conceivable that, if the reporters had been knowingly uncovering serious wrongdoing or threats to public safety, they might have been able to argue that the hacking was justified, but to date no such argument has been put forward even in a single case relating to the *News of the World*.

The cover-up

That a group of reporters on one national newspaper should have routinely adopted criminal methods to pursue stories is shocking, but it does not prove that there was something wrong with the culture of the press as a whole. If that was all that had gone wrong, other journalists, editors and proprietors in the national press, and even in News International, might have been justified in claiming that they were untainted and were entitled to carry on as before. But they cannot make that case. The sequence of events that followed the public exposure of hacking at the *News of the World* left no doubt that the press had a problem that was deep and general. It starts with the reaction of News International.

In 2006 Mulcaire and the *News of the World* royal editor, Clive Goodman, were caught hacking and arrested. They pleaded guilty and were sentenced to six and four months' jail respectively. Why others involved in hacking were not prosecuted is a matter to which we will return, but the fact that only one reporter was exposed and punished at that time made possible the cover-up that followed. It is astonishing in retrospect, but for almost four years after the convictions of Goodman and Mulcaire the company insisted to the public, to its shareholders, to Parliament, to the Press Complaints Commission (PCC) and to anyone else who would listen that Goodman was a 'rogue reporter' whose hacking activity had been a secret and unlicenced operation utterly unknown at the time to his colleagues or superiors. The company stance on this was never defensive. No matter how much doubt was cast on its story, it took the fight to its critics. When the *Guardian* exposed the Gordon Taylor hacking story, News International declared that this was 'selective and misleading journalism' and that the paper had 'substantially and likely deliberately misled the British public'. When the Commons media committee cast doubt on the company's version of events, the *News of the World* announced that the MPs had been 'shamefully hijacked' by Labour members with an axe to grind, while a company statement said the report was full of 'innuendo, unwarranted inference and exaggeration'. When the *New York Times* weighed in with a long exposé of hacking, News International's reaction was that the American paper had undermined its own reputation with dodgy reporting driven by commercial rivalry. In July 2010 it announced: 'All of these irresponsible and unsubstantiated allegations against the *News of the World* and other News International titles and its journalists are false.'

The record shows, however, that from an early date senior people at News International were aware of evidence suggesting that Goodman was one of several hackers at the *News of the World*. They were told at least four times in two years:

1. September 2006: barely a month after Goodman's arrest a senior executive of News International was briefed on the case by a Metropolitan Police officer. The information, which was passed to at least two other executives, included the following:
   - detectives already knew that more than 100 people had been hacked;
   - in some cases there had been large numbers of intercepts;

- police believed that journalists other than Goodman were involved;
- the victims included people in politics and show business (of no interest to a royal editor).

2. January 2007: at the sentencing hearing for Mulcaire and Goodman at the Old Bailey, Mulcaire's counsel stated in open court that Goodman was not the only *News of the World* reporter his client dealt with on hacking matters. Discussing the hacking of the phones of the football agent Sky Andrews and the publicist Max Clifford, barrister Neil Saunders said: 'This information would have been passed on, not to Mr Goodman – I stress the point – but to the same organization.' Addressing Mulcaire later, the judge, Mr Justice Gross, repeated the point: 'As to counts 16 to 20, you had not dealt with Goodman but with others at News International.'

3. May 2007: after his conviction Goodman was sacked for gross misconduct (though he was paid £90,000 severance). On his release from prison he challenged this as unfair, writing that 'other members of staff were carrying out the same illegal procedures' and had not been sacked, and that hacking 'was widely discussed in the daily editorial conference'. Several senior News International executives saw or were briefed about his letter.[4] (Goodman subsequently received a further payment of £153,000 from the company. Mulcaire received a payment of £80,000.)

4. June 2008: Gordon Taylor, named as a hacking
   victim in the prosecutions of Goodman and
   Mulcaire, sued News International and secured
   disclosure of documents. When the company (or
   rather its subsidiary News Group Newspapers)
   saw these documents it asked a barrister, Michael
   Silverleaf QC, what he thought of them. This is
   what he wrote: 'There is overwhelming evidence
   of the involvement of a number of senior NGN
   journalists in the illegal enquiries into
   [REDACTED]. In addition there is substantial
   surrounding material about the extent of NGN
   journalists' attempts to obtain access to information illegally in relation to other individuals. In
   the light of these facts there is a powerful case
   that there is (or was) a culture of illegal information access used at NGN in order to produce
   stories for publication.'[5]

Despite this knowledge, the company insisted to the
Commons media committee (2007 and 2009), the Press
Complaints Commission (2009) and the readers of its various papers (throughout) that there had only ever been one
rogue reporter. If challenged, executives angrily protested
that the company had conducted no fewer than three
internal investigations to see whether anyone else had
been involved, and they had all found nothing. The first
of these was run by solicitors Burton Copeland, described
as 'probably the leading firm in the country for white-
collar fraud'. 'They were given absolutely free range to ask
whatever they wanted to ask,' declared company lawyer
Tom Crone. 'My understanding of their remit was that

they were brought in to go over everything and find out what had gone on ...' Then a 'new broom' editor, Colin Myler, conducted his own investigation. MPs were told in 2007: 'Colin had come in from New York, a very experienced editor with a clear remit to do two things: make sure that any previous misconduct was identified and acted upon and that the prospect of any future misconduct would be ruled out.' MPs asked if it was 'a full, rigorous internal inquiry', and the answer was yes. The third investigation came after Goodman made his claim that hacking had been common knowledge at the paper. The PCC recorded Myler as saying that 'an email search was conducted involving up to 2,500 separate email messages in order to discover whether other *News of the World* staff were aware of the Goodman/Mulcaire criminal activity'. An independent firm of solicitors assisted with this inquiry and nothing was found.

Who could ask for more, was the company's attitude. Or as Myler put it to MPs: 'I have never worked or been associated with a newspaper that has been so forensically examined ...' In April 2011, however, News International was finally obliged to change its tune. It announced: 'It is now apparent that our previous inquiries failed to uncover important evidence and we acknowledge our actions were not sufficiently robust.' In other words, there had never been any rigorous investigation. Such inquiries as had taken place, it was now clear, had found nothing more or less than what executives had wanted them to find. The media select committee's verdict in 2012 was forthright: 'Corporately, the *News of the World* and News International misled the Committee about the true nature and extent of the internal investigations they professed to have carried out in relation to phone hacking; by making statements they would have known were not fully truthful; and by failing to disclose documents which would have helped expose the truth. Their instinct throughout, until it was too late, was to cover up rather than seek out wrongdoing and discipline the perpetrators, as they also professed they would do after the criminal convictions. In failing to investigate properly, and by ignoring evidence of widespread wrongdoing, News International and its parent News Corporation exhibited wilful blindness ...'[6]

The other cover-up

There can be no doubt, therefore, that the problem at News International was not a simple 'rotten apple' one, but was cultural. Wrongdoing did not stop with a few reporters who hacked; it extended upwards. Senior figures in the company had a choice between, on the one hand, effectively cleaning their journalistic stables and, on the other, relentlessly insisting that nothing was wrong, and they eagerly chose the latter. It is striking that not a single hint has emerged in all these years to suggest that there was internal debate about this choice. So the managers were wilful too. But here again you might hesitate. You might say that their conduct, shameful as it was, need not indict the national press in general. This was just Rupert Murdoch's company and indeed just one newspaper out of four in his stable, plus a few executives. Alas, that argument does not hold water, for the problem did not stop there. While News International was lying to the world it had many accomplices and they were powerful.

Notably, it enjoyed the energetic support of the editors and proprietors of those newspapers that were supposed to be its bitter commercial rivals.

We have seen how the other papers reacted to the Milly Dowler revelation in 2011 – by attempting to bury the story. This was a pattern. Another example is their response to the report issued by the Commons media committee in February 2010, also a landmark in the scandal. Although the MPs roundly condemned News International for 'collective amnesia', the *Daily Mail*, the *Daily Express* and the *Daily Mirror* could find no room for the story on their front pages. The *Mail*'s inside-page coverage concentrated on the committee's more technical findings on libel law, while the *Mirror* ignored the story altogether. *The Times*, meanwhile, tucked its report away on page 15. This pattern has been analysed. The academics Judith Townend and Daniel Bennett have calculated that from 2006 up to the end of 2010 – the point at which News International decided the game was up – the *Guardian*, which was making the running, published 237 articles on hacking. The tally for the *Mail* and *Mail on Sunday* between them, by contrast, was just thirty-eight articles, and the tally for the *Mirror* and *Sunday Mirror* (which were supposedly fighting tooth and nail for readers with the *Sun* and *News of the World*) was a mere eleven stories. That is eleven stories on hacking in four and a half years.[7]

Can this difference be explained in terms of reader interest? In other words, was hacking just a broadsheet-type story of no concern to tabloid readers? Hardly. People who normally obsess the tabloids were at the centre of this scandal: Jude Law, Charlotte Church, Steve Coogan ... It turned out that Prince William and Prince Harry had been hacked too; indeed it was the hacking of Prince William's voicemails that led to the conviction of Clive Goodman – a terrific story, you might think, but editors decided that this was one royal event they would not make a fuss over. As for Sienna Miller, before the scandal broke she had only to change her hat to warrant a spread in the tabloids; now, even though a leading global corporation had trampled on her rights and she was bravely standing up to it, they just weren't interested. Nor were they taken with the national security dimensions of the hacking of voicemails of cabinet ministers and senior police officers, or the alarming implications of the hacking of the phones of the most secret and closely guarded people in the country, those in witness protection. None of these did the editors feel was exciting enough to turn into a spread, or a front page, let alone a campaign – even when the *Guardian* or the *Independent* or the Commons committee or the *New York Times* did all their spadework for them. As for mounting investigations of their own into hacking, digging up sensational new facts as they tell us they love to do, it never happened once.

Editors and proprietors of the *Mirror* papers, the *Mail* papers and the *Express* papers may never actually have agreed in so many words that they would do their best to bury the hacking story, but try to bury it they did.

It is a truism that the cover-up is often worse than the original offence. The editors' conspiracy of silence is an essential part of the hacking cover-up and it certainly scores high for moral turpitude. If the scandal at News International had taken place in, say, a political party, or Barclays Bank, or the Football Association, or British Airways, there would have been no hesitation in devoting front pages to it day after day. Hacking was a scandal involving illegal activities by well-paid employees of one of the country's best-known companies, a subsidiary of a vast, foreign-owned global corporation. The *Guardian* exposed a corporate cover-up, the *New York Times* revealed more about it and the parliamentary committee did its best to shame executives for dissembling. Better still in news terms, the shadow of scandal also fell upon the police and on politicians, and celebrities were caught in the middle of it. In any other circumstances this was a perfect case for papers to print their biggest and bitterest headlines, to unleash the leader writers, the columnists and the cartoonists, to compete to be the most outraged and most self-righteous title on the newsstands. But no, they ignored it, or at best shuffled it to page 18.

This was an abuse of power by people who boast that they hold power to account. It has been rightly pointed out that editors are defined by what they don't do as much as by what they do. 'A newspaper can create great controversies, it can stir up argument within the community, discussion, it can throw light on injustices – just as it can do the opposite: it can hide things and be a great power for evil.'[8] Rupert Murdoch spoke those words in a BBC interview in 1968, and here, forty-odd years later, was an example of a gang of newspapers collectively exercising that 'great power for evil'. This alone is proof of a deep flaw running through the national press, proof that there is something rotten in the press culture.

There is much more

The natural next question is, why? Why, in the famously dog-eat-dog world of the national press, were the dogs so docile, so kind to each other? Why did only one dog (the

Guardian) bark? And the answer can only be that editors feared their own operations would not bear scrutiny. Did they also hack phones? There have always been grounds to think it would be surprising if some of them did not. For one thing it was remarkably easy to do, and it yielded results. All you had to do, really, was have the idea and have the means to get the numbers. As we shall see, they all had that means. Then only moral scruples and fear of the law would stand in the way. For another, the hacking at the *News of the World* seems to have gone on for at least six years, in which time, inevitably, a number of reporters left jobs at the Murdoch paper to work for rival titles, some of them surely taking with them knowledge of, or at least suspicions about, the hacking technique. Once they got to their new newsrooms, how likely is it that they would have kept the *News of the World*'s tricks a secret? By the time Leveson adjourned his hearings he had still heard no outright proof of hacking at other papers, but as we shall see there were plenty of clues, and some editors had admitted they could not be certain it had not happened on their papers.

Even if papers such as the *Mail*, the *Express* and the *Mirror* never hacked, they had good grounds for hoping that the public would not catch sight of the methods they employed in pursuit of stories. This brings us to Operation Motorman. Mulcaire is not the only private investigator whose revealing records of dealings with national newspapers have found their way into the hands of the authorities. There is also Steve Whittamore. There are twenty British national newspapers, including Sunday titles, and Whittamore worked for fourteen of them, including every tabloid. He worked most frequently for the *Mirror* and *Mail* papers. According to the Information Commissioner's Office (ICO), which seized his files during Operation Motorman in 2003 before he was prosecuted and convicted along with three of his associates, this is how he earned his living:

> The information which the detective supplied to the newspapers included details of criminal records, registered keepers of vehicles, driving licence details, ex-directory telephone numbers, itemized telephone billing and mobile phone records, and details of 'Friends & Family' telephone numbers. The secondary documentation seized at the same premises consisted of the detective's own hand-written personal notes and a record of work carried out, about whom and for whom. This mass of evidence documented literally thousands of section 55 offences, and added many more identifiable reporters supplied with information, bringing the total to some 305 named journalists.

Many whose personal information was accessed were prominent in one way or another, including Kate Middleton (now the Duchess of Cambridge) and her sister, Pippa, Lenny Henry, Charlotte Church, the head of MI6 and no fewer than eight England footballers. But as with phone hacking, many targets had no public role. Some were victims of crime or disaster, or their associates, including:

- relatives of two people killed in the Dunblane massacre;
- relatives of Holly Wells, murdered in Soham in 2002;
- a victim of the New York 9/11 attacks;

- a survivor of the 1999 Paddington train crash;
- relatives of Milly Dowler;
- relatives of Sarah Payne, murdered in 2000.

Other targets had no reason to believe that any newspaper would be remotely interested in their personal information, including:

- the sister of the partner of a local politician;
- the mother of a man once linked romantically to a *Big Brother* contestant;
- the mother of a woman in show business (Whittamore had details of the mother's telephone calls and records of her financial transactions);
- a painter and decorator who once worked for a lottery winner;
- a hearing-aid technician consulted by a famous person.

The scale of Whittamore's activity was remarkable. His ledgers cover just three years but according to a detailed analysis by ITN they contain more than 17,000 entries for (that is, fifteen per day) with at least 4,000 target individuals named. The *Daily Mail* alone paid him £143,150 in connection with 1,728 requests, which were, as ITN put it, potentially illegal, while the *Mail on Sunday* paid him £62,025 for similar requests. Meanwhile the *Mirror* paid him £92,000 for nearly 1,000 requests and the *People* paid £76,000 for 1,016 requests.[9]

Some of Whittamore's inquiries, such as identifying householders from published electoral rolls, were no doubt lawful, but it is clear that he was also breaking the law, and frequently. So, were the journalists who asked him for information also acting illegally? It is certainly illegal knowingly to commission someone to acquire data from, for example, the Police National Computer, the car registration (DVLA) database and the British Telecom database of people's 'Friends & Family' (or most-dialled) numbers. The files contain hundreds of requests of this kind, and thousands more requests for information that is not publicly available including ex-directory phone numbers and the addresses belonging to particular phone numbers. The Data Protection Act states that journalists who pay for such information do not break the law if they can show that the action was justified in the public interest. Exactly what that means may be subject to some argument, but it could not normally include acquiring information in the pursuit of stories about the private lives of celebrities, their relatives or the victims of crime and their families. Richard Thomas, the Information Commissioner whose team investigated Whittamore, declared: 'I have not seen a whiff of public interest.' Thomas's report on the affair stated damningly: 'At a time when senior members of the press were publicly congratulating themselves for having raised journalistic standards across the industry, many newspapers were continuing to subscribe to an undercover economy devoted to obtaining a wealth of personal information forbidden to them by law.'

The publisher of the *Mail* and the *Mail on Sunday*, Associated Newspapers, told the Leveson Inquiry that by 2011 it had investigated its past relationship with Whittamore. It questioned the reliability of the private investigator's ledgers and stated: 'We have seen no evidence that any of our journalists ever asked Mr Whittamore to do anything illegal or were aware that he might be obtaining information for them in an illegal manner.' It also said that its journalists 'used Mr Whittamore primarily to obtain addresses and telephone numbers that he could obtain more quickly and reliably than they were able to'.[10] The paper, however, confirmed that it would not dispute at the inquiry that there was prima facie evidence that journalists had acted in breach of the law by obtaining information which could not be justified in the public interest, which, as Leveson indicated, would allow him to reach his own conclusions as to the culture, ethics and practices of the press.[11]

At the very least, Motorman tells us that there was nothing unusual about the *News of the World*'s relationship with Glenn Mulcaire; indeed several national papers were routinely relying on private investigators. The money involved gives a measure of the importance of such people. Whittamore's firm received nearly £90,000 a year from the *Mail* papers alone. The *News of the World* paid Mulcaire £849,470 in eight years, meaning that this ex-footballer with no qualifications earned more per annum than the paper's experienced royal editor. We know of others too, including Jonathan Rees. In 2005, after his release from a seven-year prison sentence for conspiring to pervert the course of justice, Rees was re-engaged by the *News of the World* and paid £150,000 a year.[12] Whatever Rees was doing, therefore, it was more valuable to the newspaper even than the contribution of Mulcaire.

There can be little doubt that much of the information acquired for newspapers by these people, whether legally or illegally, was often used to support aggressive further intrusions into privacy. The practices of doorstepping and stalking – as described for example by HJK and Sienna

Miller – require phone numbers, addresses and car registrations, which was exactly what Whittamore supplied. Phone hacking also requires those numbers; indeed one of many questions still unanswered is to what extent numbers traced by Whittamore were used to hack voicemails. And the covert activities do not stop there. Since early 2011 the Metropolitan Police have been investigating not only hacking but also other forms of data intrusion by the press, including email hacking, and as of August 2012 they were dealing with 101 allegations and had arrested and bailed six people.

Returning to the question of why most of the national newspapers entered into a conspiracy of silence about hacking at the *News of the World*, the Motorman evidence confirms the answer: they all had something to fear if their reporting methods came under scrutiny. Hacking at Murdoch's Sunday tabloid was not isolated; it was part of a culture of professional privacy intrusion on or beyond the borders of legality that stretched across most of the national press. Newspapers often write of the public's right to know; it is clear that editors and reporters felt they had a right to know whatever they wanted to know about whoever crossed their paths, no matter how vulnerable and powerless those people were.

Serial libel

Just three months after Goodman and Mulcaire were jailed – an event which some hoped would serve as a warning to the national press about acting legally and responsibly – three-year-old Madeleine McCann went missing in

Portugal. If the hacking scandal and Motorman exposed the unethical and sometimes illegal methods that some newspapers used in gathering information, then the McCann case revealed a breathtaking recklessness in the writing and publishing of news.

A year on, at the High Court in London in March 2008, the *Daily Express*, the *Sunday Express*, the *Daily Star* and the *Star on Sunday* collectively apologized for publishing 'extremely serious yet baseless allegations concerning Mr and Mrs McCann over a sustained period' and agreed to pay them £550,000 in damages. As the McCanns' lawyer explained, in a sample period between September 2007 and February 2008 these papers had between them published 110 articles, many of them on their front pages, suggesting among other things that the couple had murdered their own daughter, disposed of the body and then engaged in a series of further deceptions on the police and the public. Some articles also cast doubt on the relationship between the couple, on their morality and on the genuineness of their religious faith.

In July 2008 the McCanns sued Associated Newspapers, publishers of the *Daily Mail* and (at that time) the *Evening Standard*, in relation to eighty-five articles. As Gerry McCann later explained to the Leveson Inquiry: 'The complaint was resolved with the payment of a substantial donation to be used in the search for Madeleine, and the publication of an apology by the *Evening Standard*. While the *Daily Mail* agreed to carry a number of free adverts (or appeals for information) on behalf of the Find Madeleine campaign in their contintental editions, they were not willing to publish an apology. The *Mail* resisted on the basis that they had published a number of articles which

were supportive of us which they believed largely balanced the articles reporting allegations and suspicions
about us.' In other words, he said that the *Mail* did not
deny publishing allegations and suspicions it could not
justify.

Gerry McCann and his legal advisers have said they
could have sued every national newspaper group and won.
No one has disputed this claim, and Peter Hill, who edited
the *Express* at the time of the serial libels, has agreed with
them. It is impossible to guess at the emotional impact on
parents, already acutely distressed by the disappearance of
their child, of being falsely accused of murdering their
daughter. That it went on for months and months, at a
time when they were trying to encourage police and the
public to search for Madeleine, makes the subsequent calm
and restraint of the couple remarkable. The *News of the
World* editor, Colin Myler, once bullied them into giving
an interview they did not want to give on the grounds that
they owed a debt to the paper for publicizing their case.
Later, he published long extracts from Kate McCann's
personal diary, claiming the paper had permission when
it did not. Kate McCann described to the Leveson
Inquiry the sense of violation she felt as she read her private thoughts in the tabloid. And she described the
anxiety that goes with knowing that her younger children can still, today, see repeated on internet websites
the lies conjured up by the newspapers that have since
apologised.

The McCanns were not the only victims of the collective loss of self-control by the press. The *Express* papers
also paid £375,000 in damages, and made a full apology
and retraction, to a group friends of the McCanns (who

had been referred to as the 'Tapas Seven') for allegations made against them in twenty articles. And Robert Murat, a British man living in Portugal, and two of his associates sued no fewer than ten newspapers in relation to almost 100 seriously defamatory articles, and received a reported £600,000 in damages. Again the papers – the *Sun*, the *Daily Express*, the *Sunday Express*, the *Daily Star*, the *Daily Mail*, the *Evening Standard*, the *Metro*, the *Daily Mirror*, the *Sunday Mirror* and the *News of the World* – admitted they had printed falsehoods and apologized.

Let us take stock of that. An industry supposedly haunted by financial pressures paid out probably more than £2 million in damages to a dozen people because it had published an astonishing tally of more than 300 libels against them over a period of nine months. And, as Gerry McCann pointed out, many other libels – probably hundreds more – went unprosecuted. The four *Express* group papers were the worst offenders but the *Mail*, the *Mirror* papers and the Murdoch tabloids played their parts. It was, in short, an industry-wide failure, and a cynical and knowing one. All journalists, from junior reporters up to editors, are required to know libel law, and all national newspapers employ legal experts to advise them, and yet somehow they libelled again and again and again. And they were warned: there was public criticism of the press coverage from an early date in the press itself, notably from the former *Daily Telegraph* editor Max Hastings, who wrote: 'I hang my head in shame at what our trade, as well as the Portuguese police, has made of the McCann story.'[13] In August 2007 Gerry McCann spoke in a televised interview about 'huge amounts written with no substance' and 'absolutely wild speculation'. And the couple, through lawyers, repeatedly appealed to papers to check things more carefully.

What were the consequences of this catastrophic failure, and what lessons were learned? There were no consequences. So far as is publicly known, not a single journalist was so much as given a formal warning, let alone fired, for writing lies and making up stories about innocent people. Nor did a single editor resign. Asked by MPs who at the *Express* papers had been reprimanded, editor Peter Hill replied: 'I reprimanded myself, because I was responsible.' No external body took responsibility either. The PCC, having sat on its hands for months while newspapers behaved so monstrously, also failed to investigate afterwards what had gone wrong. So no lessons were learned.

We can be certain about that failure to learn lessons because three years later the papers did it again. Around New Year of 2010/11 retired teacher Christopher Jefferies was subjected to treatment very similar to that meted out to the McCanns and Robert Murat, with similar results. He was arrested in Bristol on suspicion of murdering his tenant Joanna Yeates, and for three days he was monstered by the press. He was 'weird', 'creepy', 'lewd', 'a loner' and 'obsessed by death', according to the *Sun*. One day the paper reported he was a homosexual and the next that he had stalked a blonde woman. For the *Daily Mirror* he was a gay, dirty, eccentric peeping Tom and a friend of paedophiles. The *Mail* called him 'Mr Strange' and 'Wizard', wrote that he introduced pupils to macabre books and alleged that he had deserted his dying mother. The *Star* and the *Express* and the Sunday papers followed similar lines, and when Joanna Yeates's grieving boyfriend, Greg Reardon, lent his support to Jefferies and challenged the morality of the press, the *Mail on Sunday*, *Sunday Mirror* and *Sunday Express* chose not to mention this fact to their readers.

Jefferies was entirely innocent (another man confessed to the murder) and he sued. The result, again, was a collective apology in court, this time by the *Sun*, the *Daily Mirror*, the *Sunday Mirror*, the *Daily Record*, the *Daily Mail*, the *Daily Express*, the *Daily Star* and the *Scotsman*, and an admission that the published allegations had been entirely untrue. The damages were reported to have been around £500,000. The *Mirror* and the *Sun* were later also prosecuted by the attorney general under the Contempt of Court Act and fined £68,000 between them. Jefferies has said that his arrest and his treatment in the press left him feeling that his real identity had been torn away and another entirely false one foisted upon him. He said: 'I don't think it would be too strong a word to say that it was a kind of rape that had taken place.' But he added that whatever he felt, it had been worse for his friends and family: one relative spoke of feeling as though she had aged 100 years in the few days when Jefferies was under attack.

The *Sun*, the *Mirror* papers, the *Express* papers and the *Mail*, which between them account for almost 7 million sales every weekday morning, managed to disgrace themselves on a grand scale at least twice in four years. You might say, if you were charitable, that they fell victim to collective hysteria that caused them to lose control. But there is another way of looking at this. The cost to a newspaper in libel damages of a front-page article suggesting or implying that Murat, the McCanns or Jefferies were killers was not very high. The *Express* group paid the McCanns roughly £5,000 per libel and Robert Murat and friends received about £7,000 per libel. The calculation in the case of Christopher Jefferies is less clear, but if the total was for three days of libellous coverage spread across eight papers, that might be around £20,000 per day – and it kept the papers lively over the quiet New Year weekend.

There is other evidence to suggest a casual, balance-sheet approach to libel and the law. Roy Greenslade, a former *Mirror* editor turned City University professor and *Guardian* blogger, has conducted a study of the overall libel record of the *Express* papers between March 2008 – the McCann payout – and January 2011, a period of thirty-four months. He found that the papers either settled or lost more than twenty-three cases. In addition, there were several published apologies and a number of censures by the Press Complaints Commission and the Advertising Standards Authority.[14] The *Express* newspapers do not seem to have been willing to learn from their mistakes. And it is worth remembering that despite all the gloom in the industry the *Express* newspapers are highly profitable.

A story told by Piers Morgan in his diary-cum-autobiography may be relevant. When he was editor of the *News of the World* he wanted to steal an interview published exclusively by a rival paper, so he shouted across the room to the house lawyer: 'Hey, Tom, how many fingers will this cost if we nick it all?' The lawyer held up five fingers, indicating maximum legal costs of £50,000. Morgan wrote: 'Fifty grand would have been well worth paying for a front page and two spreads inside and the bigger sales revenue it would bring.'

Serial libelling and neglect for the law provide further proof of deep cultural problems in the press, although, as with hacking and Motorman, newspapers have generally chosen to cover up for each other. These cultural problems are not restricted to News International, nor to the *Express* papers. They are widespread among national titles and they are not something that the press itself has done anything serious about.

Truth

In the midst of all this it is worth reminding ourselves that journalism is about truth – not an absolute, objective truth because that is not possible, but the best approximation of truth that can be managed in the time available. Reporters, in other words, are supposed to give their readers an account of the real world as they understand it, on the basis of their observations and research. If they wilfully distort, or embroider, or lie, if they make up quotes or put pressure on people to say things they don't mean, then it isn't journalism, it is fiction passing itself off as journalism, and so a fraud upon the reader. Because journalism is hurried and journalists are human there will always be mistakes and misjudgements, and when they occur they should be swiftly acknowledged and corrected. Equally, the truth will always be contested and journalism should always be open and fair about that, reporting other perceptions of the truth where they arise. And if challenged on facts, a journalist should be ready to defend his or her work with evidence.

Whatever the complexities, that basic principle, that journalists try to express the truth as they see it or understand it, is unshakable. And if it sounds pious, if the mere conjunction of the words 'truth' and 'journalism' is enough to make you snigger, then that is a measure of how badly things have gone wrong. It is also a reaction that suits dishonest journalists, who need you to accept low ethical standards and to be as cynical as possible about what gets published. With other people who have important jobs we tend to have high standards. We expect doctors to try to heal, accountants to try to get the numbers right and firefighters to try to fight fires, and when they fail to do those things we are usually shocked and angry. We should not expect less of journalists than that they try to tell the truth.

In this context it is worth looking at the kind of activity that leads to the publication of gross falsehoods in the press. The case of Max Mosley is often another cause of sniggering, but it is also a flagrant example of how journalists can treat truth with contempt. Mosley was the president of the Federation Internationale de l'Automobile and so an important person though a little-known one in Britain. (When the story about him arose, the *News of the World* newsdesk had to be referred to Mosley's Wikipedia entry to tell them who he was.) He is also the son of Oswald Mosley, the fascist leader. Max Mosley had for years engaged in sadomasochistic role-play parties in which he paid some or all of the other participants, and this was reported in the *News of the World* under the headline 'F1 boss in sick Nazi orgy with 5 hookers'. He sued for breach of privacy and the trial cruelly exposed the paper's methods and approach, and in particular its attitude to truth.

- It promised £25,000 to its source, a woman participant, and then paid her only £12,000 because it knew she could not hold it to its word.

- It described the event as 'Nazi' on the basis that one participant spoke some German (she was German), even though it had not even translated what she said.

- It linked the role-play to the Holocaust on the basis that German was spoken in one role-play scenario and that someone wore a prison costume in another.

- It offered more money to its source if she 'gave an interview', which involved her signing a script already written by a reporter (which, the court heard, was later amended without her knowledge).

- It told two other participants that if they did not cooperate it would name them in print, and then in court asserted that this was not blackmail.

- It provided a series of justifications of its actions that the judge described as 'artificial', 'thought up' and 'verging on the desperate'.

- Its principal reporter on the case was told by the judge that his 'best recollection is so erratic and changeable that it would not be safe to place unqualified reliance on his evidence'.

- It lost the case, refused to apologize to anyone and claimed publicly that it deserved a journalism award for the story. No one from the editor down resigned or was disciplined.

The paper, in short, cheated a woman who helped it violate the privacy of a man who, so far from being a role model, was apparently previously unknown to its own newsdesk, and then it gave the event a Nazi angle in defiance of the evidence. It went on to bully a series of women into providing it with a signature validating a made-up interview, and presented a court with artificial justifications and a reporter who couldn't be believed. You may consider Mosley's activities strange or even immoral, but when a paper is prepared to adopt this approach to the truth it simply doesn't matter what its targets do. Christopher Jefferies was a blameless retired man living alone in Bristol, quietly participating in his local Neighbourhood Watch and the Liberal Democrat Party branch, but in the hands of national newspapers he became a homosexual, death-obsessed friend of paedophiles, a corrupter of the young, a peeping Tom and a stalker of blonde women. All of this was false. The McCanns were distraught parents a long way from home who were desperately trying to promote an international search for their missing daughter while caring for their two other children. In the hands of national newspapers they became heavy drinkers of dubious sexual morality who faked their faith and were ruthlessly and cynically covering up the drugging and killing – or alternatively the sale – of their own three-year-old child. This too, as the worst offenders have admitted, was false. And it doesn't stop with personal reputations. There is plenty of evidence to show that the same reckless attitude to truth is sometimes applied to the coverage of politics and public affairs, with consequences that are in their way just as damaging.

Self-regulation

Mosley, the McCanns and Jefferies all sued and won, and all of them testified to the Leveson Inquiry that the victories hardly began to compensate them for the distress and the damage to reputation they had suffered. For the majority of people who have fewer resources or less spectacular grounds for complaint, however, even the limited satisfaction of going to court is not available. Those people will always need another form of redress that is cheaper, simpler and quicker, and this brings us to the Press Complaints Commission.

The PCC has few defenders today. The consensus is, as David Cameron put it in July 2011, that 'the Press Complaints Commission has failed'.[15] But the word 'failure' does not quite do justice to the problem, because it could be inferred that honest effort was involved; that people tried and did not quite succeed. The story of self-regulation over six decades is not like that. The staff of the PCC may well have done their best, and they may have brought satisfaction to many who complained, but institutionally this is a story of deception in which editors and proprietors doggedly frustrated public opinion and the will of parliament while exploiting the press megaphone to suggest that something very different and noble was going on. The story of self-regulation, in fact, is further proof of a general, cultural problem in the national press, and particularly at the top of the national press.

The early years of the story went like this:

- 1949: The first royal commission on the press told the industry to set up a self-regulatory General Council of the Press. The industry did nothing.
- 1953: After MPs threatened to take things into their own hands the industry finally created the Press Council, but it was a far weaker body than the royal commission had suggested.

- 1962: A second royal commission gave the industry another chance to make self-regulation effective. Some changes followed, but the Press Council continued to be seen 'more as a champion of the press than as a watchdog for the public'.
- 1969: The Younger committee on privacy recommended reform of the Press Council. The industry took four years to act and then implemented only some changes.
- 1977: The third royal commission demanded change and threatened a statutory solution if it did not come. Again, only a grudging minimum of changes was made.
- 1983: The independent Robertson report on the Press Council recommended major changes. They were not made.

Bear in mind that none of these commissions and inquiries came out of nothing. Usually they were the result of alarm at the conduct or the state of national newspapers, often following a steady build-up of scandals and abuses that outraged public opinion. Usually, too, they reflected exasperation at the industry's failure to address its own problems. Every inquiry urged editors and owners to put their own house in order and recommended measures to be taken. And every inquiry stopped short of recommending parliamentary intervention, although in several cases such action was threatened. In 1953 it was a private member's bill proposing a statutory press council that forced owners and editors to act. When the General Council of the Press was created that year, the Labour MP C. J. Simmons agreed to withdraw his bill but told the

Commons: 'I give warning here and now that if it fails, some of us again will have to come forward with a measure similar to this bill.' In 1962 the second royal commission declared: 'We think that the Press should be given another opportunity itself voluntarily to establish an authoritative General Council ... We recommend, however, that the government should specify a time limit after which legislation would be introduced.'

Cleverly, the industry's leaders dodged the bullets. Where they made concessions – on lay representation in the Press Council, on providing more money for it, on establishing a code of practice, on improving its complaints operation – it was always minimal and always late. They perfected the art of dragging their feet to the point where official patience was about to snap and then making the smallest possible concession needed to avoid action against them. Sometimes the concessions were not even real ones, or were never actually implemented. And always the message bellowed down the megaphone at the newspaper-reading public was that the Press Council was a fine and effective body, that press standards were steadily rising and that all those who challenged this Panglossian view were enemies of free speech. Warnings of last chances meant nothing.

This was the depressing background to David Mellor's 1989 remark about the Last Chance Saloon. At that time there had just been a series of press scandals of a familiar character, of which the siege of the hospital deathbed of television presenter Russell Harty was one. Harty had been outed as gay by the press, which was then desperate to prove he had AIDS. The result was described at his memorial service by his friend Alan Bennett: 'Reporters intermittently infested his home village for more than a year, bribing local children for information about his private life, even (there is a terrible comedy in it) trying to bribe the local vicar. Now he fought for his life in St James's Hospital; one newspaper took a flat opposite and had a camera with a long lens trained on the window of his ward – the nurses would point it out to you when you visited him. A reporter posing as a junior doctor smuggled himself into the ward and demanded to see his notes, and every lunch-time reporters took the hospital porters over the road to the pub to try to bribe them into taking a photo of him.' Another scandal in Mellor's mind, no doubt, was the *Sun*'s reporting of the Hillsborough Stadium disaster of April 1989, in which ninety-six people died. The paper alleged on its front page that drunken Liverpool fans picked the pockets of the dead and urinated on them, and that they attacked rescue workers. It wasn't true and it caused such outrage in Liverpool that to this day many in the city will not touch the paper.

What followed was the Calcutt committee on privacy and related matters, a behind-closed-doors review of the state of the press and of the Press Council, chaired by the barrister Sir David Calcutt QC. In a noteworthy moment during the meetings, Rupert Murdoch is reported to have appealed to the committee to give the press another chance. 'Another chance?' asked a sceptical member, aware of all the previous squandered chances. Murdoch insisted that this time the press really would do better. And, remarkably, the committee appears to have believed him. Its report called for the closure of the Press Council and its replacement by a Press Complaints Commission, but the new PCC would be another self-regulatory body, funded by the industry and with no element of statutory backing, though Calcutt demanded that it should have independent leadership.

While he gave the press another chance, Calcutt also laid down that the new body must be seen to work well, and if that didn't happen it should be replaced with something statutory. The Conservative government of the time welcomed the report and Home Secretary David Waddington issued a warning along similar lines: 'This is positively the last chance for the industry to establish an effective non-statutory system of regulation.' This time, he declared, the threat was not an empty one: 'If maverick publications decline to respect the authority of the press complaints commission … that triggers off the next step. Calcutt recommends that, in those circumstances, the press complaints commission should be put on a statutory basis, and we have accepted that recommendation.' For the Labour opposition, Roy Hattersley responded: 'The Home Secretary expressed the belief that newspapers will respond to this one last chance, I have my doubts. That is why the second major implication and recommendation of Calcutt – the introduction of statutory regulations by an official body – is absolutely essential if the year of grace is ignored and if the press do not mend their ways.'[16]

So what happened next? The Press Council was scrapped but when the editors and owners came up with their design for a PCC it was a mere shadow of what Calcutt had called for. Built in to the Calcutt findings, as the Home Secretary had noted, was a requirement for a progress report on the PCC. Calcutt himself conducted this and he reported in 1993. He found the following:

The Press Complaints Commission is not, in my view, an effective regulator of the press. The Commission has not been set up in a way, and is not operating a code of practice, which enables it to command not only press but public confidence. It does not, in my view, hold the balance fairly between the press and the individual. The Commission is not the truly independent body which it should be. The Commission, as constituted, is, in essence, a body set up by the industry, financed by the industry, dominated by the industry, operating a code of practice devised by the industry and which is over-favourable to the industry.[17]

What was supposed to have been the final last chance had been offered, taken and once again wasted, and it was time for parliament and government to take responsibility. In place of the PCC, Calcutt recommended a statutory complaints tribunal. By now, however, the passage of time was playing its traditional role. The head of steam that led to the establishment of Calcutt's inquiry was long in the past. Public outrage had subsided and thanks to an intervening election the Conservative majority in parliament was greatly reduced. Ministers who had been so firm in 1990 now ducked what they knew would have been a tough confrontation with the press. First they delayed again by carrying out a review of Calcutt's review, coming up with different proposals. Then the whole idea of press reform was shelved. The PCC was allowed to carry on.

The PCC

Two decades later, the PCC's record is as dismal as Calcutt would have predicted, and his account of its shortcomings is seen to be eerily telling. Although it was consistently presented to parliament and the public as a regulator, it was no such thing. It was a moderately successful complaints agency, although even in that role it had significant flaws. It was supposed to raise standards but where it succeeded was only in areas that did not impinge upon the power and prerogatives of the editors. And any external criticism of the PCC was always drowned out by the megaphone while any concessions were usually minimal and grudging.

Perhaps the most dramatic failure was in the McCann case. From the disappearance of the little girl in May 2007 to the *Express* surrender and apology in March 2008 the PCC uttered not a single word of public criticism of the coverage. Nor did it issue private warnings. This in a period when, as we have seen, hundreds of libels were being published and when public criticism of the papers was loud. Technically, we have been told, a series of catch-22s protected the editors. The McCanns did not want to alienate the press generally because they knew papers could help in the search for their daughter, so for a long time they were reluctant to take action of any kind, either in the form of mounting a complaint to the PCC or a legal suit for libel. At the same time the PCC famously would not welcome complaints about the coverage from anyone other than those directly affected: in this case the McCanns. In the absence of any acceptable complaint, therefore, the PCC said or implied that it was unable to act. (In fact, the PCC's articles of association allowed it to mount investigations on its own initiative, but it almost never did this.) So it did almost nothing. It did not even complain about its own powerlessness, but sat and watched as the false McCann stories mounted up. (And it could have had no doubt that at least some of the stories were false, not least because they so often contradicted one another.) Once the McCanns finally sued the *Express* early in 2008 the PCC had another excuse for inaction: it did not allow itself to delve in matters already before the courts. It was only when the *Express* paid up and apologized that the PCC suddenly developed an opinion: the chairman, Sir Christopher Meyer, said the paper was a disgrace. But still nothing was done, no inquest was conducted into this spectacular failure of standards and no lessons were learned.

With phone hacking the story was different but the outcome the same, in that the PCC's conduct suited the editors. When hacking was first revealed in 2006 the commission made some recommendations to its members in an effort to ensure the practice was not repeated, and after the *Guardian* made its first serious revelations of a more widespread problem in 2009 it broke with tradition and set up an investigation. Alas, this was a feeble affair and, on the basis of the same evidence that led the Commons media committee to conclude that the *News of the World* had a serious case to answer, the PCC declared that it had no case to answer. Instead, the PCC managed to accuse the *Guardian* of exaggerating its discovery – a conclusion that other newspapers gratefully and enthusiastically reported. That PCC report was withdrawn only in July 2011, months after even News International had abandoned its 'one rogue reporter' story.

As Calcutt predicted, even where its structure was not already biased in favour of editors (they alone wrote the code and controlled the money, and they participated in adjudications, albeit not where their own paper was concerned) the PCC tended to give the press the benefit of the doubt. It was reluctant to entertain complaints by anyone other than people directly affected. It would rarely accept complaints from groups, which meant there was little to inhibit newspapers from maligning all Muslims or all Roma people (as they so often like to do). A reader who paid good money for a newspaper and found its front-page story to be utterly false would have difficulty taking a case to the PCC, although a citizen who merely sees (but does not pay for) a misleading advertising billboard is encouraged to complain to the Advertising Standards Authority.

Equally, the press as regular users of the PCC service (unlike ordinary members of the public) became adept at 'gaming' the system. It was advertised to the public as a lawyer-free service, yet some papers regularly assigned PCC cases to their in-house lawyers – inevitably rendering the struggle more unequal. It never held hearings, so when a journalist and a complainant disagreed on important facts it was more or less paralysed. And the PCC's focus on quiet mediation, which in one sense was admirable, had the side effect of concealing breaches of the code. Cases rarely went all the way to formal adjudication by the commissioners, and so newspapers were rarely asked to publish formal verdicts where complaints were upheld and they were found to be at fault. Nor were breaches of the code automatically recorded wherever they were found. The resolved or settled cases – frequently the equivalent of 'guilty pleas' and often the most egregious – were not reported as 'convictions' by the PCC let alone the newspaper. This could leave papers looking well-behaved even if they were not. In the case of the *Daily Mail*, as the Media Standards Trust discovered:

> In 2010 there were sixty-three substantive complaints made to the PCC against the *Daily Mail*. In forty-seven of these the *Daily Mail* appeared to admit to a Code breach (by correcting or apologizing for the story), yet in the whole of 2010 there was not one upheld complaint against the *Daily Mail*. In other words, even though the *Daily Mail* may have breached the Code almost on a weekly basis, it looked as though it had an entirely clean record.[18]

Editors often spoke of how much they hated having an adjudication against them. If that was true, then perhaps more adjudications would have led to more lessons being learned; but as the years went by the PCC supplied fewer and fewer – the number fell from 142 in 1989 to just forty-four in 2010, even though the number of complaints had tripled. The PCC was even more reluctant to use its power of investigation, and on the rare occasions it did it could probe only as deep as editors chose to allow, and where it found fault it had no power to sanction. It claimed to raise standards progressively, through the influence of its adjudications, but even after it had been operating for a decade and more the press was still capable of the mass, serial falsehoods of the McCann case, of the mass purchase of illegally acquired private information, and of the outrage that was hacking.

All this time the editors, with rare exceptions, claimed that the PCC was a powerful regulator, that it did a great job, that they lived in fear of its rulings, that their reporters kept its code in their wallets and purses and that no better model of press regulation could be found anywhere in the world. As recently as January 2009 — after Motorman, the conviction of Clive Goodman and the McCann affair — the various organizations representing the editors of Britain's newspapers and magazines made a submission to the Commons media committee that contained the following bold statements:

- 'There is no doubt that ... standards of reporting have been raised markedly since the PCC and the Code were established in 1991. Change has been incremental; but on very many issues ... it has been very significant';
- 'Self-regulation has inculcated within our industry a culture of correcting inaccuracies and other breaches of the Code speedily and effectively';
- 'The PCC itself has proved to be an efficient and accessible regulator';
- 'The PCC and self-regulation work well, and it is difficult to discern any grounds for its fundamental tenets to be questioned'.[19]

The MPs on the media committee, reporting in February 2010, unanimously rejected those views and (like so many well-meaning bodies before it) put forward a programme for reform. Without departing from the principle of self-regulation it called for the creation of a standards arm of the PCC, capable of conducting investigations and ensuring that lessons were learned. It said the PCC should be able to impose fines. And it suggested the organization be renamed the Press Complaints and Standards Commission to make its new mission explicit. All of these proposals were angrily rejected both by the industry leadership and by the PCC itself. It was only after July 2011 that the need for change was acknowledged, and by then some change was certain to come whether the editors and owners wanted it or not.

From its inception the PCC was less a genuine regulator than a confidence trick, perpetrated upon the British public and parliament by editors and proprietors who wanted to protect their operations from scrutiny and criticism. When Calcutt appeared to have them cornered in 1990 they created an organization that had the appearance, but only the appearance, of what he proposed, and they exploited their reliable ally, time, to neutralize the 1993 review that was meant to make them conform. It is a story repeated time and again over the sixty-year history of their battle against accountability. The victims of this deception are all of those people who since 1990 have been abused by the press and have not had effective redress, and you can read many of their stories in the submission to the Leveson Inquiry of the Media Wise Trust.[20] The victims are also the public at large, which has not had the quality of newspaper or of journalism that it deserves and needs. If further proof were needed, the story of self-regulation and the story of the PCC provide it: the national press needs change, and it cannot be trusted to carry out that change itself. There must be no more last chances.

The Leveson Inquiry

All of this – hacking, Motorman, the McCann and Jefferies cases, the shortcomings of the PCC and more – was known before the Leveson Inquiry opened its doors on 14 November 2011. The inquiry sat for nine months and received evidence from 474 people and 135 organizations. The briefest summary of it all is this: overwhelmingly it confirmed the picture painted above – that amidst the good journalism in the British press there is plenty that disgraces the industry, and that the industry's leaders had failed to tackle the problem. From thousands of stories told to the inquiry, here is a small selection.

The Watsons

Margaret and James Watson told the inquiry that after their daughter, Diane, was murdered in 1991 inaccurate press reporting implying that she bore some responsibility for her own death contributed to the suicide of their fifteen-year-old son, Alan. When his body was found he had copies of the articles in his hand. They described how their son had become distressed by the reports, and how they took him to a solicitor who explained that nothing that is written about the dead counts as libel. Margaret Watson said: 'I'm afraid that all just became too much for Alan. And I don't blame him because I can understand. So the journalists in this country kicking on about the chilling effect if you do away with the Press Complaints Commission – which you have to do away with – that if you do away with the Press Complaints Commission it will have a chilling effect on journalists. What about the deadly effect it has on the victims and misreporting, the malicious lies, the malicious falsehoods? Just because a person's deceased, you can write what you want, and they certainly did it.' Asked about an article published on the day Alan was buried, she replied: 'I thought at least they would leave us alone for Alan's funeral. They took away his respect, they took away his dignity, and the very day that we were laying our son to rest … If you say that's good journalism, if any journalist thinks that's good, God forgive you, because I won't.'[21]

Charlotte Church's mother

As part of an intensive operation against the Welsh singer, who was just sixteen when it began, the *News of the World* hacked her phone and the phones of her mother, Maria, and stepfather, James. Church said reporters 'totally immersed' themselves in her life and has alleged that the paper published thirty-three hacking-based news stories about her in four years. One story in 2005 revealed that her stepfather had had an affair and had taken cocaine. Shortly before that was published her mother, who had known about the affair and knew the article was being prepared, attempted to take her own life. Church told the inquiry: 'It just had a massive, massive impact on my family life, on my mother's health – which the *News of the World* had reported on before then – on her mental health state and her hospital treatment, which we also think the only way they could have known about that hospital treatment, etc., was either through the hacking or possibly through the bribing of hospital staff, etc. So they knew how vulnerable she was and still printed this story.'

In her written statement Church described the sequel: 'The *News of the World* put a proposal to my mother. The proposal was that *News of the World* wanted an exclusive story of her breakdown, self-harming and attempted suicide in exchange for not printing a follow-up story about my father's infidelity. My mother gave them the exclusive interview, which was published on 18 December 2005. She felt she had no choice other than to play by their rules. The follow-up story of my father's sex life was then published in the *People* the next week anyway. This sequence of events drove my mother to additional self-harming and had a dramatic impact on her mental health. The havoc that the press have created within my family has been devastating.'[22]

Spitting photographers

Sienna Miller described what it was like to be pursued by photographers: 'For a number of years I was relentlessly pursued by about ten to fifteen men almost daily, pretty much daily and, you know, anything from being spat at or verbally abused. I think that the incentive is really to get as strong a reaction as possible, so – you know, as other people have mentioned – but being jumped out at, when you get a shock, or saying things to kind of get some emotional reaction. They seemed to go to any lengths to try to upset you, which is really difficult to deal with.' She went on: 'I would often find myself – I was twenty-one – at midnight running down a dark street on my own with ten big men chasing me and the fact that they had cameras in their hands meant that that was legal, but if you take away the cameras, what have you got? You've got a pack of men chasing a woman and obviously that's a very intimidating situation to be in.[23]

Hidden Motorman

Peter Wright, then still editor of the *Mail on Sunday*, told the inquiry in his statement: 'As editor I am responsible for all the content of the *Mail on Sunday* and for the behaviour of all of our journalists while working for the paper.' He went on to explain: 'I was unaware of the use of inquiry agents until we heard of the Information Commissioner's investigation.' By that time, according to research by ITN, his paper had spent £62,000 on potentially illegal searches by Steve Whittamore.[24] Wright wrote that he missed this expenditure because of an unusual accounting arrangement: 'For budgetary purposes I have since 2003 monitored payments to journalistic contributors prepared by department editors on a weekly basis. Payments to inquiry agencies for research and information were classed with payments for taxis, flights, accommodation, etc., and were monitored by our managing editor. I rebuked him for failing to alert me to the practice of employing inquiry agents.' Wright later insisted in testimony: 'I don't think there was any deliberate attempt to conceal them.'[25]

Letter in a schoolbag

The author J. K. Rowling described to the inquiry her efforts to protect her children from press scrutiny. She explained: 'As an adult I have made certain choices in my life and I must accept that certain consequences follow. However, my children have not made any such choices. I consider that they should be allowed to enjoy a normal childhood in which to grow and develop as people in peace, without outside interference by the media.' Rowling recounted an incident involving her elder daughter: 'She was in her first year at primary school and I unzipped her school bag in the evening and among the usual letters from school and debris that every child generates, I found an envelope addressed to me and the letter was from a journalist. It's my recollection that the letter said that he intended to ask a mother at the school to put this in my daughter's bag ... I know no more than that. I don't know whether that's how the letter got in my daughter's school bag or not, but I can only say that I felt such a sense of invasion that my daughter's bag ... It's very difficult to say how angry I felt that my five-year-old daughter's school was no longer a place of, you know, complete security from journalists.'

An editor investigated

The inquiry heard that the *Express* papers continued to employ Steve Whittamore until July 2010, five years after he had been convicted. (The *Daily Mail* employed him until 2007.) In one instance from 2007 the *Express* paid £963.50 to Whittamore for work in relation to 'P. Wilby', almost certainly Peter Wilby, a former editor of the *Independent on Sunday*. Days before, Wilby had written in the *Guardian* about the coverage of the McCann affair and remarked that the *Express* was 'a hopeless newspaper that couldn't tell you the time of day'. At that time £963.50 was almost exactly the price for four full days' work by Whittamore, raising the possibility that Wilby – whose address and phone details could be found in the public directory – was placed under surveillance because he had mocked the paper. The *Express* editor of the time told the inquiry he was 'not aware of ever having used a private investigator at the *Daily Express*' though he added that he could not speak for his subordinates.

Text message

On 7 October 2009 the chief executive of News International texted David Cameron, who was about to address the Conservative Party conference: 'But seriously I do understand the issue with the Times. Let's discuss over country supper soon. On the party it was because I had asked a number of NI people to Manchester post endorsement and they were disappointed not to see you. But as always Sam was wonderful – (and I thought it was OE's that were charm personified!) I am so rooting for you tomorrow not just as a proud friend but because professionally we're definitely in this together! Speech of your life? Yes he Cam!'

Corruption

Deputy Assistant Commissioner Sue Akers, the police officer in charge of investigating hacking and related matters, gave evidence in February and July 2011, and mentioned in particular her detectives' work on corruption of officials by journalists. By February sixteen journalists had been arrested and bailed by this team, including staff at the *Sun* as well as the *News of the World*. Her statement said: 'There appears to have been a culture at the *Sun* of illegal payments, and systems have been created to facilitate such payments whilst hiding the identity of the official receiving the money.' She said it was clear that journalists knew that what they were doing was illegal and that '… the authority level for such payments to be made is provided at a senior level within the newspaper'. Akers continued: 'The cases we are investigating are not ones involving the odd drink, or meal, to police officers or other public officials. Instead, these are cases in which arrests have been made involving the delivery of regular, frequent and sometimes significant sums of money to small numbers of public officials by journalists. Some of the initial emails reveal, upon further detailed investigation, multiple payments to individuals of thousands of pounds. In one case the figure, over several years, is in excess of £80,000. There is also mention in some emails of public officials being placed on "retainers" and this is a line of inquiry currently being investigated. One of the arrested journalists has, over several years, received over £150,000 in cash to pay his sources, a number of whom were public officials.'[26]

In July Akers returned to reveal that twenty-three journalists had been arrested and bailed in connection with possible illegal payments and investigations by then extended to include journalists at papers in the *Mirror* and *Express* groups. Payments totalling nearly £35,000 appeared to have been channelled to one prison officer from News International, Trinity Mirror and Express Newspapers, while a second prison officer appeared to have received more than £14,000 from the *Daily Mirror*, with payments made up to January 2012. The stories apparently generated by these payments, Akers said, 'reveal very limited material of genuine public interest'.

A death that wasn't

The editor of the *Daily Star*, Dawn Neesom, was asked about her paper's headline policy, in particular a front-page headline announcing the death of Simon Cowell:

> Answer: Our front pages have to be as eye-catching as we can make them. 'Telly king Cowell is dead' in particular was a quote from Gary Barlow, and obviously – you only have a finite amount of words you can fit on a page one … I believe the exact quote was – and obviously Gary Barlow was only joking, because that's the nature of their relationship – 'As far as we're concerned, Cowell's dead,' as far as the show was concerned, and that is explained in the sub-deck and the copy. But yes, it was designed to be an eye-catching headline.
>
> Question: Yes, to create as much impact as possible in order that the person passing the newspaper stand might say, 'I'll buy the *Star* today.' Is that correct?
>
> A: Yes.
>
> Q: Even though, if one was going to be pernickety about it, if not slightly pompous about it, it's wrong, isn't it?
>
> A: Um … it's dramatic. Eye-catching.
>
> Q: The next one: 'Terror as plane hits ash cloud' … There was no plane hitting an ash cloud, was there?[27]

Anonymous evidence

In January 2012 Associated Newspapers, publishers of the *Daily Mail*, went to the High Court to argue that the Leveson Inquiry should not be allowed to take evidence from anonymous witnesses on the grounds that this would be a breach of human rights law. It argued that if journalists were allowed to testify without giving their names, the reputation of the *Mail* might be tarnished by evidence whose merit could not be tested. Lord Justice Leveson had said he was approached by some journalists who feared they would lose their jobs if they gave critical evidence about papers. Three judges threw out the *Mail*'s case. The *New Statesman* writer Steven Baxter commented: 'It's deliciously hypocritical of the *Daily Mail* to use the "Yuman Rites Act" it has so often pilloried in the past to attempt to stop others from using the kind of anonymous sources it wouldn't think twice about using.'[28]

Pretend journalist

Derek Webb, a retired police constable turned private investigator, testified that over a period of eight years the *News of the World* commissioned him to carry out surveillance on around 150 people, including two lawyers acting for people who were suing the paper over hacking. Other targets included a police superintendent and the Director of Public Prosecutions. After the arrest of Mulcaire for hacking in 2006 Webb was told by the *News of the World* that they would continue to employ him only if he gave up his private investigator's licence and joined the National Union of Journalists. He did as they asked, though he told the inquiry that he was never a journalist.

Watching the detectives

In 2002 David Cook was part of a Metropolitan Police team investigating the murder of Daniel Morgan, a private investigator and the business partner of Jonathan Rees, who was employed extensively by the *News of the World*. After Cook made an appeal about the Morgan case on the BBC's *Crimewatch* programme, the *News of the World* began a surveillance operation against him and his then wife, Jacqui Hames, also a police officer. Their phones were hacked, they were placed under surveillance (Cook was followed as he walked his children to school) and the paper acquired information about Hames's work record, which, she told the inquiry, could only have come from police files. When the couple complained, according to Hames, neither the Metropolitan Police nor the *News of the World* showed a serious interest in getting to the bottom of this, the paper claiming that it had been trying to find out whether Cook and Hames were having an affair. They were married. Hames told the inquiry she believed that the *News of the World* had put her and her husband under surveillance because 'suspects in the Daniel Morgan murder inquiry were using their association with a powerful and well-resourced newspaper to intimidate us and try to attempt to subvert the investigation'.

Hacking and the *Mirror*

Former *Mirror* journalist James Hipwell told the inquiry that mobile phone voicemail hacking was once 'bog-standard procedure' on the show-business desk of the *Daily Mirror*. Hipwell, who was jailed in 2006 for his part in a share-tipping conspiracy, said he himself had been taught the technique at the paper. Piers Morgan, who edited the *Mirror* up to 2004, was asked at the inquiry whether hacking went on at the paper then and replied: 'I don't believe so.' Pressed on the point, he said: 'To the best of my recollection, I do not believe so.' Another perspective was supplied by Jeremy Paxman, who testified that at a lunch at *Mirror* headquarters in 2002 Morgan had described to him how to hack a phone. Someone working on the *Mirror*'s show-business desk in those years was Dominic Mohan, later editor of the *Sun*. In 2002 the paper won an award sponsored by Vodafone and when Mohan accepted it he thanked what he called 'Vodafone's lack of security'. Mohan told the inquiry he had said this 'purely as a joke' and that he had known about hacking only from industry rumours. Piers Morgan's successor as editor of the *Mirror*, Richard Wallace, told the inquiry: 'I am not aware of any deliberate transgression of the criminal law at the *Daily Mirror* that has arisen during my time as editor.'

The Bowles family

Sebastian Bowles, aged eleven, was one of twenty-eight people killed in a coach crash in Switzerland in March 2012 while returning from a ski trip. His father, Edward, mother, Anna, and sister, Helena, aged nine, were staying in a Swiss hotel designated for bereaved families when Edward and Helena were photographed from a distance. They were on the doorstep of the hotel, waiting to be taken to see the body. Both were holding flowers and Edward Bowles was comforting his daughter, who was crying. (At about the same time, reporters had gathered on the doorstep of their home and were questioning neighbours about the family.) This photograph, along with other family photographs taken without permission from Edward Bowles's Facebook site, were published on the websites of some newspapers, as were photographs and extracts from a ski-trip blog site, also reproduced without permission. The *Daily Mail* was one of these papers. Mr Bowles complained to the *Mail* through his solicitor, Giles Crown, and through the PCC, and the paper took down the Facebook pictures – though it said they had been 'openly accessible', a point Mr Bowles disputed. The paper did not remove the photograph of the grieving Helena from its website and it was still there three months later. When the *Mail* finally took it down it said it had not known that the picture, which had been taken by an agency and which was cropped to exclude Edward Bowles's face, was of Helena. Mr Crown, giving evidence to the inquiry on behalf of Mr Bowles, argued that the paper was in no doubt about the family's wishes and could easily have established the identity of the girl in the picture. The PCC code bans the photographing of children under sixteen years of age without parental permission, and it also requires discretion and sensitivity in the reporting of grief and shock. The inquiry noted that these events happened while its hearings were in progress.

What is to be Done?

National newspapers are not the first industry to go through a crisis of this kind, and they will not be the last. Their difficulties coincide, for example, with the difficulties of the banks, and there are some similarities between the problems of the two and between the likely solutions.

Just as the vast majority of bank employees and executives are undoubtedly honourable people who work hard, care about the public and would not dream of behaving unethically or illegally, so it is with journalists. If your newspaper runs to sixty-four pages every day it is likely that most days of the week all or nearly all of those sixty-four pages display material that would not have raised an eyebrow of suspicion, let alone of criticism, for anyone at the Leveson Inquiry. This does not mean, however, that society should turn a blind eye on the minority of occasions when things go wrong, either in banks or in newspapers. That would be like saying, after a poorly maintained passenger airliner has crashed, that we will overlook it because thousands of other flights operated by the same company have landed safely. The world is not like that, as newspapers would be the first to point out. When things go wrong we need to know, for a start, what mistakes were made and (usually) who made them. Then we have to know whether the problem arises from something general in that organization. And we also need to be reassured that responsibilities are taken and lessons learned, because otherwise it will just happen again.

With the banks there has been a fairly consistent diagnosis since 2008 (outside the banking sector at least) that leadership has been bad and that sick cultures have developed further down the system. As a director of the Financial Services Authority put it to MPs, describing Barclays at the time of the Libor rate-fixing affair: 'There was a culture of gaming. It had to change.' And: 'You could not escape the conclusion that the culture of this institution was coming from the top.'[29] So with newspapers there is no escaping the conclusion that there is a big problem, a problem of culture: we know this because of hacking, the News International cover-up, the conspiracy of silence among rival papers, the Motorman affair, serial libelling, the designed-in shortcomings of the PCC and much more. And as with the banks much of the responsibility must rest with those at the top – those who own and run the newspapers and who encouraged the development of unhealthy cultures or failed to correct them. Changing a culture is difficult. With the banks the consensus is that better regulation will make a difference. And so it is with the press, where weak regulation has both contributed to the problems and been a symptom of them.

Regulation

There has been no shortage of proposals for better ways of regulating the press. The Leveson Inquiry must have received around twenty, while it also considered other approaches used in other countries. No 'model' is perfect (very little in the public realm is perfect) but several were promising. Hacked Off did not support any one scheme; instead it has asked for the same things it asked for when it launched: effective regulation that is independent both of the industry and of government and that provides swift, accessible redress for victims of abuse. A regulator should be able to bear down on bad journalism and promote the good. We have some basic tests for identifying a system capable of making a positive difference, and the first of those tests is that it must be independent of the editors and proprietors, who led their industry into its present crisis.

We cannot possibly, as a society, give them another 'last chance' to conjure up yet another ingenious vehicle for what has been called 'self-interested regulation'. If those decades of experience tell us anything, it is that the people who run the national press have squandered the right to be trusted. Had it been otherwise there would have been no need for a public inquiry, or indeed for the fistful of other press inquiries that preceded it. Of course the press should have a role in its own regulation, but even then there is no reason to restrict that role to editors and proprietors – 'the press' comprises more than them. But whatever happens now the press, and especially its leaders, must not be left as the final judge in its own trials, nor should it own and operate the courtroom, write the rule book, pay the lawyers and select the jury. The people running the regulator, if it is to command public confidence, have to be unequivocally independent by background and in mode of appointment, and also manifestly free of influence.

The second test is that the regulator and those running it must be independent of any other vested interest, including government. There should be no question of the regulator becoming an instrument of ministers or MPs or political parties, so the independence of those running it must include independence from all of these – and equally from any possible corporate influence. Journalism should not be accountable to vested interests or it could find itself serving those interests rather than the interests of the public at large.

Third, the regulator must provide effective redress to those who can show they have been wronged by the press. There are various ways of doing this and a mix might be appropriate: some mediation, some arbitration and some adjudication. What counts is that it should be fair, cheap, transparent and swift.

Fourth, it should have the ability, resources and authority to mount investigations where there is concern among the public or in the industry that press journalism is causing or has caused unjustified harm. The investigators should have the power to require disclosure of documents and testimony from relevant witnesses. They should identify lessons to be learned, and their findings, conclusions and recommendations should be published.

And fifth, the regulator should have clout. It should be able to impose meaningful sanctions in cases where there has been serious wrongdoing.

To these five, we need to add another. A regulator, especially if it is to impose sanctions, must have the power to compel membership. There is no point to regulation, in other words, if significant organizations publishing journalism can choose not to be subject to its authority or can walk away rather than pay a fine. In the late 1980s the *Sunday Sport*, then a significant title and one prone to reckless and unethical journalism, did not belong to the Press Council. It was one of the changes promised at the creation of the Press Complaints Commission that this problem of opting out (known as the 'Sullivan problem', after the *Sport*'s publisher, David Sullivan) would be solved, yet in recent years it has arisen again, as all four papers in the *Express* group have rejected the authority of the PCC. We have moved from the Sullivan problem to the Desmond problem (Richard Desmond being the owner of the *Express* group).

And finally, there may be a further test, because we almost certainly need a mechanism for keeping the regulator virtuous. Another lesson of the past is that a new regulator beginning work after a period of heightened public concern might seem effective and fair at first, but after a few years of dealing directly and consistently with one industry it may 'go native', developing habits and reflexes that together amount to institutional bias. This is all the more likely if the industry is footing the bills. One way of placing a check on this might be annual external audits by an external body with the authority to enforce compliance with fixed standards.

These, then, are seven criteria for a regulator:

- independence from editors and proprietors;
- independence from other interests including government;
- the ability to provide redress;
- the ability to investigate when things go wrong;
- the ability to impose sanctions;
- the ability to compel membership;
- regular submission to external inspection.

A regulator with all seven of these might command public trust and might really have the power to prevent abuses and raise standards. Other tests could be applied, but this seems to be a working minimum.

Hacked Off believes that for a regulator to pass those seven tests, legislation will be required. In our view the compulsion of membership, the power of sanction, the external audit and the mechanisms for independent appointments all demand the backing of statute. As the jargon has it, therefore, we favour 'statutory underpinning' for press regulation. This is emphatically not placing the press under the thumb of politicians; it is merely ensuring that the new regime can be sufficiently robust to make a difference. It can be done without compromising independence: as Lord Justice Leveson pointed out several times during his public hearings, it is by statute that we have a system guaranteeing the independence of the judiciary, which is no less vital to our democracy, and that independence is maintained to general satisfaction. Something similar can be achieved with a press regulator.

The proposals of the editors and proprietors

Among the proposals put to the Leveson Inquiry was one presented on behalf of editors and proprietors by Lord Black of Brentwood, who is executive director of the *Telegraph* papers, chair of the Press Standards Board of Finance (PressBoF) and a former director of the PCC. (PressBoF is the body that has funded the PCC, and it has been the chief vehicle of influence for the national paper managements.) Lord Black's proposal is the scheme the national papers (with a few possible exceptions) can be expected to cling to and promote whatever happens, for months and possibly years. It represents the least in terms of concessions that they believe they can get away with in their present crisis.

Even if it had no other flaws, the Black plan was inevitably suspect because of its provenance, since the editors and proprietors have lost our trust. As we have seen, for decades they claimed the right to design their own regulation and they consistently failed to produce anything credible. Worse, they are guilty of denying the failings of self-regulation when these were pointed out, of having attacked and abused their critics, and of having boasted instead that what they had was the envy of the world. As recently as 2009 they were telling us this. And as recently as the spring of 2011 they had no intention of changing the PCC at all. On this basis, we are entitled to approach their proposals with the same caution we would apply to the patter of a cold caller from a company that has already sold us several bad deals.

Unsurprisingly the plan does have other flaws. Though Lord Black calls it 'independently-led self-regulation' its chief innovation is not its leadership but its system of contracts. Members would be bound in by five-year contracts, meaning that they would be legally obliged to conform to the rules and to pay fines when they breached them. This sounds good (it was a suggestion put forward by one of the royal commissions and was rejected out of hand by papers at the time), but it falls apart when you think about it. For one, it does not solve the old Sullivan problem, now the Desmond problem: that key industry players may opt out. Contracts are by their nature voluntary and companies may choose not to sign, or they may sign and then at the first time of asking decide not to renew. Lord Black insists that everybody who counts would sign now, but even if that were certain it is not especially reassuring. All contracts have at least two parties, so a powerful newspaper group might claim at some stage that the new regulator had breached its contract, so forcing an ugly rupture. Equally, when contracts came to be renewed they might be rewritten; certainly nobody could guarantee that they might not be. Contracts, in other words, are not effective means of compelling membership or imposing authority.

As for independence of leadership, the Black plan involves a Trust with a chair, who is a key personality. How is that chair chosen? By an appointments panel with two lay members (from outside the newspaper business) and two members representing the industry. This was the exchange when Lord Black was asked about his plan at the Leveson Inquiry:

Q: But how is that system independent of press interests, given that (a) unanimity is required, and that (b), there are two industry members on the appointments panel?

A: It is because it's a balance. Neither the public members nor the press members have control of it, so I think it is, in the terms of the draft criteria, sufficiently independent of the industry to be clear that it is not an industry appointment.

Q: But a strong-willed industry representative could simply veto anybody who they didn't think would serve their interests.

A: And vice versa, sir.

Q: Well, it's true, but the independent people who are

coming into it presumably from a different perspective will not have quite the same command of the subject and will not be quite as aware of all the potential ramifications as the MPA [industry] representatives, will they?

A: I think it will be incumbent on the trust board to make sure the individuals it puts on there are authoritative figures who can command that sort of interest and knowledge.

Q: But one way of doing that, therefore, might be to say: it's a majority.[30]

The key problem revealed in this dialogue is that the editors and proprietors can't bring themselves to relinquish control. Even if they were to tinker with their plan, that much is established by the first draft. They continue to believe that they are entitled to regulate their own affairs and that the public is not entitled to anything better than what they, the editors and owners, are prepared to offer. They therefore try to finesse real independence and external accountability and they also reject any idea of statutory underpinning. They make concessions – an investigations arm, the possibility of heavy fines – but without real sacrifice of power. They must be answerable to no one. In other words, they have not learned from events since 1990 and they are hoping to pull off again today the trick they pulled off back then.

But they are not fools. In all but that fundamental respect – who has power? – the Black scheme can be made to seem impressive, and it has the propaganda power of the megaphone behind it. Ministers and readers are told that it is a ready-made solution to the problems of the past few years, and that the sensible thing to do is give it a try.

That way we will all avoid a bitter conflict from which no one can benefit. What they do not say is that if there was conflict it would be of their making because they stand almost alone in resisting meaningful change. They do not say that giving them what they want would be renewing their lease on the Last Chance Saloon. They do not say that it would expose many innocent people in the future to the abuses we have seen in the past. They do not say that letting them have their way again would be like saying to the country's leading banks: 'You have lost a fortune gambling our money, so here is another trillion pounds to waste.'

Failing the Cameron test

In his testimony to the inquiry, David Cameron explained twice what he thought would be the real test of a new regulatory regime for the press. 'I will never forget meeting with the Dowler family in Downing Street to run through the terms of this Inquiry with them and to hear what they had been through and how it had redoubled, trebled the pain and agony they'd been through over losing Milly. I'll never forget that, and that's the test of all this. It's not: do the politicians or the press feel happy with what we get? It's: are we really protecting people who have been caught up and absolutely thrown to the wolves by this process?' Later he said: 'I think we've discussed the overall challenge and that's what we need to meet, and we should, as I say again, bear in mind who we're doing this for, why we're here in the first place, and that's the real test. If the families like the Dowlers feel this has really changed the way they would have been treated, we would have done our job properly.'[31]

At the very end of the inquiry hearings, the 'core participant victims', or CPVs, who included in their number the Dowlers, the McCanns and Jacqui Hames, made a written submission giving their views on what they had heard. This is what they had to say about the regulation proposals put forward on behalf of the editors and proprietors: 'The Module 4 CPVs all agree that the proposal advocated by Lord Hunt and Black for a new contractual self-regulatory body would not be a satisfactory solution. The proposal is considered to be an insufficiently clean break from the current PCC and the failings associated with that organisation. In the event that this system was established, it is anticipated by the Module 4 CPVs that complainants would be likely to prefer court proceedings as a forum for seeking redress.'[32]

The role of an effective regulator

Much of what a new and effective regulator would do is obvious from the tests, but it is worth filling in some more of the picture.

- It would address complaints relating to a clear, new code of conduct, ensuring some parity of arms between complainants and publishers so that, as far as possible, fairness could prevail.
- It would mediate, arbitrate or adjudicate as appropriate, and without fear or favour; and it would be frank and open with the public about the outcomes of these procedures.

- It would provide redress where complaints were upheld, including requiring the publication of prominent corrections and apologies.
- It would also seek to learn lessons – and more importantly ensure that the newspaper learned the lessons – when things go wrong, and to ensure that responsibility is assigned and acknowledged. This might relate to a single complaint or to a wider issue such as the McCann affair. In the latter case, once it was clear there was a problem, investigators would establish the facts and then, perhaps, issue public warnings or, after the event, make recommendations for changes to procedure. Such changes might, for example, involve ensuring that editors kept abreast of particular aspects of their operations, or that reporters consulted more with their superiors on the sourcing of their reports.
- It would have the power to accept third-party complaints.
- It might also involve advising papers to be more frank with readers about the quality of their news sources.

Besides these, the regulator would write and maintain a new code of practice for journalists, and for this there should probably be a discrete code committee made up of editors, journalists, experts (for example, ethicists) and a minority of independent members representing the interests of the public. The regulator would also intervene early to advise and if necessary protect people caught in media storms, and would require editors to call off reporters where code breaches were occurring. It would do things that many regulators do, serving an educational function, promoting best practice, monitoring and advising on relevant legal and social change, commenting in relevant public forums, promoting its own services and generally engaging with the industry and the public to improve practice and raise awareness of significant issues.

With all of this, the public would experience a noticeable change. The importance and thus the profile of the new regulator would be higher than at present and its rulings and statements, coming from a truly independent source and backed ultimately by sanctions, would inevitably carry more weight. Members of the public would have more confidence in such a regulator, and, over time, perhaps more trust in papers, which would be more likely to adhere to the spirit and letter of the code.

What would it mean for journalists? For many, one consequence would be that they would be asked more often, and would have to ask themselves more often, whether what they were doing was ethical. The code of practice would no longer be, as it has been, merely an instrument compiled by the people who were already their bosses, but would become something with a standing of its own. And given that the code would be mainly the work of professionals, it would reflect the thinking and practical understanding of professionals, so it would be a practical document. At the same time journalists would know that the regulator had the power of investigation, so, for example, they would need to keep good records. (In principle this is nothing new: journalists have been taught for decades that they should retain their notes for at least a year.) This might in the modern context involve attaching to their submitted copy data files of recorded interviews, links to websites and emails. It would probably also involve records of consultations with news editors and lawyers, showing that due care was taken. To some journalists this might sound cumbersome and slow, but it is technically relatively easy today and it is also no more in terms of bureaucracy than is required of doctors and police officers, who also often have to work fast and whose work is also important. To some journalists it might sound prissy and fussy. To them the only answer is that decades of paying insufficient attention to ethics has caused harm to the lives of many people and has brought journalism into disrepute. This way is better.

While many may doubt that journalists are capable of a cultural change of this kind, there is a recent precedent. A generation ago it was a given in the national press that many people drank large quantities of alcohol during working hours, and that reporters routinely fiddled their expenses. Both were subjects of amusement and even pride across the industry, indeed at least half of all journalism's favourite anecdotes in those days were drink-related. The ability to write or edit while drunk was sometimes held up as a measure of professionalism, just as fake expenses claims were regarded less as petty crime than as a right – and the more brazen the claim the bigger the boast in the pub afterwards. Now that has changed, not least thanks to Rupert Murdoch, who astonished Fleet Street by banning alcohol from his Wapping editorial offices and who has never liked other people being free with his money. Drunkenness on duty and shamelessly inflated expense claims are now exceptions in the industry, and what is more most modern journalists don't miss them and would not defend them. If anything, that is a bigger cultural change than the ethical upgrade that is now required.

The public interest

When journalism hurts people it sometimes owes them an apology and perhaps compensation. On other occasions, however, journalism may be right to hurt people: they may deserve it. How do we know the difference? And, more important, how would a regulator tell the difference? Those are big questions when we speak of encouraging the development of a better culture for journalism.

Often it is easy for a journalist to justify hurting, upsetting or annoying people. If somebody is shamed or embarrassed because their court conviction is made public they surely have nothing to complain about. Court verdicts are public matters and there is an ironclad argument that the public ought to be informed about them. The same is true when politicians are shown to be taking money in exchange for influence: the politicians may not like it but it is their actions that are wrong, not the reporting. In both cases the journalists could say that although they may have upset some people they were serving the public interest, and no reasonable person would dispute that. In this way the idea of the public interest operates as a shield for journalism, a precious protection it can have as it goes about its business. In some circumstances, even journalists who break the law are formally entitled to invoke the public interest as a defence (while in some others they aren't entitled to, but should be). So what is the public interest?

Well, to start with, it is obviously not the same as what interests the public. Interesting the public is also a vital part of journalism and not merely because newspapers go out of business if they fail to do it: if you are a reporter with a story to tell, you must tell it in a way that people will be prepared to read. But entertaining readers and satisfying their curiosity could never *on their own* justify the kind of journalism that harms people. That would legitimize all kinds of gratuitous cruelty and dishonesty, reviving the morality that permitted bear-baiting and public executions. Put simply, newspapers can't hurt people just for fun, no matter how much their customers might like reading about it.

The public interest is about the greater good, not about fun. Journalists must be allowed to cause harm when they do it for that greater good, or to use the plainest of words when they help make the world a better place, or help prevent it becoming a worse one. Of course when the law rules on these things or when a regulator makes an assessment the definition needs to be much more precise, but that is the spirit of the thing. And if it sounds pious so be it, because once again it is a measure of how far journalism has lost trust that the idea of it doing good can seem incongruous. This simple test involving the greater good also extends to the methods employed by journalists, which as we know can be harmful too. Is it ever right for a journalist to steal a document? It may be, if the document may provide proof of serious wrongdoing. Is it ever right for a journalist to hack mobile phone voicemails? It may be, if hearing the messages supports an article that helps to prevent serious crime.

It is often said that providing a more detailed definition

of the public interest in relation to journalism is impossible. This is not true (although it has certainly suited those wishing to abuse the concept to encourage that idea). Ofcom, the BBC and the PCC have all defined it, and they are not alone. Here is the PCC's account of the matter, which was written by editors:

1. The public interest includes, but is not confined to:
   i) Detecting or exposing crime or serious impropriety.
   ii) Protecting public health and safety.
   iii) Preventing the public from being misled by an action or statement of an individual or organisation.
2. There is a public interest in freedom of expression itself.
3. Whenever the public interest is invoked, the PCC will require editors to demonstrate fully that they reasonably believed that publication, or journalistic activity undertaken with a view to publication, would be in the public interest.
4. The PCC will consider the extent to which material is already in the public domain, or will become so.
5. In cases involving children under 16, editors must demonstrate an exceptional public interest to over-ride the normally paramount interest of the child.

Here is another formulation, from draft guidelines published in April 2012 by the Director of Public Prosecutions, Keir Starmer:

Examples of conduct which is capable of serving the public interest include the following:

a. Conduct which is capable of disclosing that a criminal offence has been committed, is being committed, or is likely to be committed.

b. Conduct which is capable of disclosing that a person has failed, is failing, or is likely to fail to comply with any legal obligation to which s/he is subject.

c. Conduct which is capable of disclosing that a miscarriage of justice has occurred, is occurring or is likely to occur.

d. Conduct which is capable of raising or contributing to an important matter of public debate.

e. Conduct which is capable of disclosing that anything falling within any one of the above is being, or is likely to be, deliberately concealed.

Neither of these, even their authors would quickly concede, is perfect for all cases. Who decides what is 'serious impropriety' or what is 'an important matter of public debate'? Editors might take different views from some of the people their reporters write about, so there is room for argument. But there is always room for argument, even in the laws relating to murder and theft. Just because we can't have perfection does not mean we can't have something very good, something which is clear and helpful in the great majority of instances even if there remain some hard cases which need to be determined on their particular merits. In other words, it is well within our capabilities to create a good, workable definition of the public interest that editors and journalists can know and rely upon and that the public and a future regulator can test them against.

There is evidence that the public already has a good grasp of the public interest. A recent poll published in the *British Journalism Review* offered a series of scenarios and asked people whether they thought they were suitable material for publication by newspapers. Where stories involved potential crimes and public health issues they were clearly considered to be in the public interest and 'ought to be published'. By contrast, a politician's daughter being drunk in public, a pop singer having cosmetic surgery and a television-show contestant having once attempted suicide were firmly considered to be private matters which should not be published. Most strikingly, nearly six out of ten people thought that a well-known England footballer having an extramarital affair was a private matter that should not be published. Such findings suggest that the public's thinking is close to the DPP's, and also to the thinking of the civil courts in privacy cases.[33]

Hacked Off argues that more of our laws, including the Bribery Act, the Misuse of Computers Act, the Official Secrets Act and the Defamation Act, should make explicit provision for public-interest defences. This doesn't mean that journalists should have get-out-of-jail-free cards, but that they should know that if they are genuinely acting for the greater good the law will protect them. Without such protection these laws may be deterring journalists from doing valuable work. By way of example, in 2011, having learned that a magistrates' court official in East London was accepting bribes to doctor a court database, the *Sun* paid him £500 to prove what he was up to. In doing so the paper breached the Bribery Act and if prosecuted would not have been allowed to mount a public-interest defence. As it happened there was no prosecution, but the *Sun* reporters could not have known that in advance. They risked jail. No doubt it reassured them to know they had a big corporation behind them, but in similar circumstances a reporter for a smaller paper or a freelance journalist would probably have dropped the story rather than take the same risk, in which case the corrupt behaviour might not have been halted.

Claiming the protection offered by the public interest is not a matter of publishing and then cobbling together a justification. It requires a proper process and once again that means keeping good records and ensuring that at every stage the right questions have been asked and were answered satisfactorily. This is already familiar to some journalists from what is called the 'Reynolds defence' in defamation cases – indeed in a Reynolds case (taking its name from a libel case brought by former Irish Prime Minister Albert Reynolds against the *Sunday Times* in the 1990s) journalists who can show they have taken appropriate care and behaved responsibly may be acquitted *even if they have got their story wrong*. The key, though, is being able to prove responsible behaviour. It is easy for journalists to underestimate the harm they can do and also to slip into the belief that they have a right to do harm whenever they think it is appropriate, and that anyone who questions them is merely trying to cover something up. But if any other profession had such power and claimed the right to use it unchecked, journalists would be the first to complain.

The press and politicians

If we are really to learn the lessons of the past few years we should tackle the problem of the relationship between the press and politicians. Once again, after our recent experiences and in particular after what emerged at the Leveson Inquiry, only a diehard few could deny that there was such a problem. Three former prime ministers told the inquiry there was, and so did the current leaders of all three main political parties. In the Commons on 6 July 2011 a chorus of MPs stood up to describe and regret the undue influence of the press, and they said very little that most members of the public had not known for years. The editors and proprietors of national papers enjoy too much behind-the-scenes influence over our politicians and what they do. Politicians have been spending too much time talking to them, accepting their favours and cultivating their good opinions, and the price for this in terms of public trust and the shape of public policy is too high. The general remedy has to be greater openness. Elected politicians and ministers may spend as much time as they like with newspaper proprietors, their executives, editors and senior journalists, so long as they declare every minute of it and explain the context. If ministers meet people in this field, other than working journalists, those meetings should also be minuted. There should be no more shufflings at the back door of 10 Downing Street followed by conversations between prime ministers and press barons that neither afterwards can quite remember or account for. As David Cameron has acknowledged by laying down new rules, such behaviour is no longer acceptable.

But there is another aspect to the problem, which demands a more specific remedy. Over the past forty years Rupert Murdoch's organization became too powerful in Britain, enjoyed too much access to politicians and, one way or another, too much influence over policy. (It is a marvel how some normally sceptical journalists will challenge that last assertion, arguing that there is no proof that Murdoch influenced policies. Do they really believe he expended all that effort cultivating prime ministers because he enjoyed their company?) Murdoch came to own a greater proportion of our national press by circulation than anyone has since Lord Northcliffe, who died a bitter megalomaniac in 1922. Murdoch also has a controlling (though minority) interest in BSkyB television, a phenomenally lucrative enterprise that has built a dominance of sports coverage, and is now seeking to do the same in drama, by the simple means of outspending all rivals. If Sky wants to own rights to a sport or the next series of a big American drama, it is almost unstoppable. That Murdoch's sustained courtship of politicians eased his passage to this powerful position can hardly be doubted. His power over them is equally obvious. His papers were the 'swing voters' in the mass-circulation market: unlike the Tory *Mail* and the Labour-leaning *Mirror*, the *Sun* could change partners. Politicians were under pressure to stay in step. So for Murdoch it was a win–win: the bigger his stake in British media the more politicians needed him, and the more they needed him the more they would help him increase his stake. Unfortunately this was a lose–lose for the public because our democracy and the diversity of our media suffered.

Murdoch's plans were frustrated at least temporarily by the hacking scandal, and his bid for outright ownership of BSkyB fell through, but that doesn't mean he will never come back for more, or that some other media organization (Google has a lot of money, and so do Apple and Microsoft) might one day try in his place. We need a cap, a limit on how much of our media, and especially our news media, any one person or company is allowed to own. This is not a controversial proposition, at least in principle, because there is almost certainly universal agreement that it would be unhealthy if any organization owned, say, 75 per cent of our news media. That would give it too much control over the information we all receive, too much ability to influence what we know and therefore what we think. So we agree on a cap in principle, but where should we set it? At 50 per cent? Forty? Thirty? Twenty? What does Murdoch have now? And how, in any case, can you calculate such a figure across the different media: print, online and broadcast? Again, Leveson heard plenty of suggestions on these questions, and workable solutions have long been available. This is not the place for the technicalities, but the principle is surely sound: that plurality and diversity in our news media is something that needs clear and formal protection, not least because an overdominant player can exert damaging pressure on our politicians in a way that is bad for everyone else.

Is This All Too Risky? No.

Freedom of expression, free public debate, the free exchange of ideas and information – these are all vital to our democracy. No less vital is the freedom of journalists to find and reveal information about government, politicians and policies, about businesses, institutions and powerful individuals, about social changes and about crime and wrongdoing. To do that job well, journalists need to be troublemakers, they need to be noisy and awkward, they need, sometimes, to have the latitude to go too far so that when it counts they have the nerve to go far enough. The last thing we need is journalists who are constantly looking over their shoulders for fear of offending. This raises the question: if we have effective regulation, a new code of practice, more accountability and serious penalties for papers that go astray, are we jeopardizing the vital benefits of free journalism? Could we find that we have created a compliant press?

The editors and proprietors of national newspapers, with just a few exceptions, would have you believe that the answer is undoubtedly yes. They argue that 'statutory regulation' (a phrase which gives the false impression that the only kind of statute available is straight censorship) will inevitably kill freedom of expression. We have no reason to take them at their word since we know they are desperately trying to protect their vested interest, trying to avoid losing some of their power, trying to cover up a record of abuses and of failure to address abuses. And yet just because those people are saying something doesn't necessarily mean it is untrue, and this is not an area where we can take risks.

This much is clear: the politicians all insist that they have no intention of endangering free expression. When Ed Miliband, the Labour Party leader, gave evidence to Leveson he said: 'There is cross-party consensus on the crucial role in our public life played by a free press. It is one of Britain's proudest traditions and fundamental to our democracy.' The other party leaders confirmed this. Nick Clegg said: 'I think a free press self-evidently is the lifeblood of a free and democratic society, and the freedom of the press needs to be protected at all times at all costs.' And this was David Cameron: 'A free and fearless press is an essential part of our democratic process and politicians must act to maintain this wider principle.' They all elaborated on their remarks in similar ways. This was the Prime Minister's version: 'The regulatory system, that's obviously the big question: what's the future for self-regulation, how do we make sure it's independent, how does it work, how do we make it robust, how do we make it compulsory, how can we make sure there are proper penalties and the public have confidence in it? All consistent with the free, vibrant, rigorous, challenging press we want to see in our country.' Ed Miliband said: 'I think it would be very important to insert in any bill constitutional safeguards on the freedom of the press. Very, very important.'

Are these just fine words? Only a fool, you might say, takes politicians' promises at face value, and there is also a slippery-slope argument here: a suggestion that even if politicians don't start by wishing to gag the press, if we grant them the means to do so, or even the beginnings of the means, then over time they will simply be unable to resist the temptation. Give them an inch now, in other words, and they will eventually take a mile. This is one of those assertions that you can't disprove, but when you review the evidence that is available you find that there is little or no support for it. After all, if British politicians really had an irresistible tendency to meddle with the press they could have done it at any time in the past half-century, yet they never did. Quite the reverse: as we have seen, the national press has repeatedly got itself in trouble and yet was always able to persuade parliament to give it another chance. Again and again parliament said this chance was the last one, and again and again the national press exposed those threats as bluff. On at least four occasions in sixty years MPs could have made a compelling case to each other and to the public that they had no choice but to take action to restrain the press, but on every one of those occasions they backed off. Far from having a fatal tendency to gag, in fact, they seem always to have been timid, and given the abuses that have unfailingly followed – for example, in the past ten years – it could be argued that they were too timid.

Another way of looking at this is to consider what happens in broadcast news and current affairs. In this country these have always been subject to what the editors and proprietors would call statutory regulation, which is to say that independent regulators (the BBC Trust and Ofcom) have been set up by parliamentary statute. So, if ministers and other politicians had a fatal tendency to interfere in journalism, and to do so more and more as time passed, the broadcast world would surely provide us with the evidence. Does it? All broadcast journalism is required by law and by the regulators to be non-partisan, which is to say that under the rules we cannot have a mainstream British broadcaster remotely like Rupert Murdoch's Fox News, or even news bulletins which reported events with a deliberate or consistent party-political slant. This is a matter of long-standing consensus. People may moan about bias in the BBC or Sky News, but their journalism passes tough regulatory tests on this and no one could claim they are anything like Fox. In a way, this is political interference with journalism, but it is hard to imagine anyone arguing that it is politicians constraining free expression. On the contrary, it opens the airwaves to the expression of conflicting ideas. (By the way, no one has suggested restricting partisanship in the British press, which has a long history of party-political advocacy.)

Are broadcast journalists at the BBC, ITV, Sky and the rest prevented from reporting matters of public interest by the regulators, and do they find themselves obliged to behave with deference towards the government of the day? The inquisitorial activities of Jeremy Paxman and John Humphrys strongly suggest otherwise, and so does more general reporting, which frequently infuriates ministers and frontbenchers. The events surrounding the Hutton Inquiry in 2003, when a BBC report was declared to have been 'unfounded' and the corporation was criticized for loose editorial processes, provide several morals. One is that the BBC broadcast the contentious item in the first place, suggesting that journalists were not afraid of the government. Another is that a public inquiry was required to investigate the government's complaint, and ministers were not simply free to sack the broadcasters as they might be if they were in real control. It was occasionally alleged in the years that followed that BBC journalists were more timid in their reporting as a result of Hutton, but BBC journalists themselves are quick to deny that, and it remains the case that BBC journalism is the most respected form of journalism in the country.

Ofcom and the BBC Trust do not provide a model for the regulation of the press because there are too many differences between broadcast and written journalism, but they do offer a guide to how politicians behave in relation to journalism that is subject to effective regulation underpinned by statute. As always what we find is not perfect, but we have something pretty good, and certainly not evidence of the kind of sustained and intensifying political meddling in journalism, or censoring of reporting, that editors and proprietors suggest is inevitable if we have regulation of the press that is underpinned by statute. Instead we have good, dynamic broadcast journalism that investigates, that challenges politicians to a degree they dislike, and that also happens to be accountable and (with rare exceptions) responsible.

It is worth noting, too, that the terms of reference of the Leveson Inquiry required it to propose solutions which guarantee the independence of the press from government. They instructed the judge, among other things, to make recommendations 'for a new, more effective policy and regulatory regime *which supports the integrity and freedom of the press, the plurality of the media, and its independence, including from Government,* while encouraging the highest ethical and professional standards'. Leveson himself never tired of reminding the inquiry hearings that he had no intention of straying from this. He remarked in one of the later sessions: 'On many occasions throughout the hearings, I have consistently and repeatedly emphasized the fundamental importance of free speech and a free press.' It is notable, too, that among the assessors appointed to advise the inquiry was Shami Chakrabarti, the director of Liberty, an eighty-year-old organization (it used to be the National Council for Civil Liberties) dedicated to, among other things, the protection of freedom of expression.

Far from proving that effective regulation inevitably places us on the slippery slope to censorship (or, as one editor put it, to Zimbabwe), the available evidence suggests that our society is perfectly capable of crafting an effective regulatory regime which bears down on journalism that causes unjustified harm without inhibiting the vital – yet often unpopular – kinds of journalism that serve the public interest. For years, editors and proprietors have frightened us with that bogey word 'statutory', but when you reflect on it statutes are usually necessary and good and are an essential part of our democracy, and they can also be subtle. Statutory regulation could mean Zimbabwe if parliament chose to pass a censorship law, but nobody is advocating anything of the kind. Instead, for example, parliament may pass a law that facilitates good regulation while explicitly placing it at a distance from, and making it independent of, government, ministers and MPs. To say that this is the thin end of the wedge is nonsense: parliament has always had the power, if it wished, to censor the press and it has not done so in the modern era. It had that power five years ago and it will have that power five years from now. We are not about to make some fatal alteration in our political system.

And remember, if we don't change there is a price to be paid. It may not be paid by me or by you, if we are lucky, but it will be paid by the people on whom, in its arbitrary way, the news spotlight falls, and who therefore risk being subjected to the kinds of treatment that made the Leveson Inquiry necessary. The press will not reform itself and it will not regulate itself in the public interest. All history proves it. So if we want to protect blameless citizens from abusive, bullying and dishonest treatment by journalists, those journalists and the people who direct them must be accountable in a meaningful way to somebody other than themselves. We cannot simply write off the future victims of press abuses as a price to be paid for press freedom, first because that is a false choice (as explained above) and second because those people have rights. They could be you or me, and they are entitled to society's protection. If you doubt this, imagine that you have a sister or a daughter in her teens who won a medal at the Olympics. Under the unwritten rules that have governed the press in the past decade, she, her relatives, her boyfriends, her coaches and her training companions would be fair game for the kind of treatment dished out to HJK, whose life was made a misery for months for no better reason than that he (or she) had dated a celebrity a few times. Every kind of spurious argument would be deployed to justify whatever intrusion into all these lives the editors thought they could get away with, and if the Olympic medallist complained, her name would be blackened and the waspish columnists would mock her looks, question her morals and call her ungrateful and spoiled. Something like this has happened again and again and it is not a manifestation of free expression but of cruelty. We have a right to be protected from it.

There are those who say that effective regulation might make our papers dull. It is an argument once embraced by the bear-baiters and the hosts of public executions, but we don't miss those things and indeed we are better off without them. And watching the ill-treatment of people such as Christopher Jefferies is not an entertainment but a deception: the readers were told that there was a case against him and so by implication he was fair game. There wasn't and he wasn't. A cruel fiction was woven around him, for public entertainment. A case has also been made that if we don't allow the popular newspapers some leeway on these matters they may go out of business, and we would end up losing diversity in our daily press. That is a little like saying that if we don't allow the building industry to cut corners on its workers' safety some companies may go bust. How many injuries on building sites would be too many? How many sacrificial victims should we allow a newspaper so that it could stay in the black?

Incidentally, while the mass-circulation newspapers may be witnessing a long-term decline in print sales, they are not on their uppers, as they seem to want the public to believe. The *Guardian*'s Dan Sabbagh summed up the position in July 2012: 'The inconvenient reality is that large chunks of the business are profitable. Tabloids continue to make healthy profits: the *Mail*'s Associated Newspapers £76m; Richard Desmond's titles £36.6m; Mirror Group £83.1m; and of course (though its profits are as yet uncounted in public) the *Sun*. Circulations are falling, but underlying sales are substantial and prices are rising to compensate – the *Sun* up 10p Monday to Friday. Even so tabloids remain relatively cheap. The complaint is more could be invested in editorial at the weaker titles, while taken together there is a profit pool of £300m.'[34] And in the unlikely event that a paper went out of business because it could not meet regulatory requirements, what would that tell us? That it could not afford to be fair and accurate? That it could not afford to check its stories? Why would we miss a paper like that?

There is one more argument against change that is worth addressing, not least because it has been put forward by the Lord Chief Justice, Lord Judge. In a speech delivered at about the time the Leveson Inquiry began work, Lord Judge said this:

> First, crime is crime. If and when crime is committed by reporters with or without the support and encouragement of an editor, it should be investigated, and if on the available evidence there is a reasonable prospect of a successful prosecution, he or they are prosecuted. We do not say that the General Medical Council and self-regulation have failed when, as sometimes happens, a doctor sexually molests one or more of his patients, or like Dr Shipman murders them.[35]

What he is saying here is that we can rely on the courts to deal with serious wrongdoing perpetrated in the name of journalism, just as it delivered justice and deterrence in the case of Harold Shipman. By implication, therefore, we may not need stricter regulation. Others have made a similar case, saying that the failures of recent years have been failures to apply the law, no more and no less. If hacking had been prosecuted properly in 2007 that would have been the end of the matter: no cover-up, no disgraced police, no Leveson Inquiry. As for the McCanns, Robert Murat and Christopher Jefferies, they sued and got lots of money, didn't they, so the system obviously works when the law is applied. Viewed in this way, everything looks different.

It is, however, a false perspective. Look at the Shipman analogy. If the courts had convicted and sentenced Shipman and he had emerged from jail to commit the same crime again, we would be wondering about the effectiveness of the law. And if, after a second conviction, he reoffended a third time, we would be demanding that the law be changed. This is what has happened in the serial libels: the same papers offend, are punished and commit the crime again. They are above the law. Now look at Motorman and the illegal inquiries commissioned by newspapers from Steve Whittamore. No journalist was prosecuted because, according to the Information Commissioner, he did not have the resources to take on national newspapers. In any case the penalties are so low that newspapers could ultimately have paid the fines from petty cash. And the penalties remained low even after Motorman, because a delegation of editors and newspaper executives lobbied the Prime Minister of the time, Gordon Brown, to ensure they were not increased. Equally, the Information Commissioner still does not have the resources to prosecute. So the law is virtually powerless. And last, look at hacking. It is true that the law was not enforced, but the evidence elicited by the Leveson Inquiry about the relationship between the *News of the World* and the Metropolitan Police was enough, if not to prove direct and deliberate collusion, then to rob us of any confidence that there was no such collusion. In other words, we are entitled to wonder whether the failure to prosecute owed more to the power of the press than to some prosecutorial mishap. All of these threads lead back to the culture of the press rather than the state of the law. It is that culture which needs to change.

As Lord Justice Leveson himself acknowledged, however, such change is by no means inevitable. The opponents of change have an impressive armoury: their megaphone; their easy political access; their influence; their money. Time always works for them, as public anger wanes and politicians lose their nerve. And as we have seen, they also have history on their side. If we are to have a press that we can trust not to lie and bully, not to use underhand or illegal methods without good reason and not to cover up its own misdeeds, then we can't just sit and wait for it because that way we will be cheated again. We have to compete with that megaphone, make known our views and show we have not simply forgotten the past victims of press abuse and all the dreadful evidence presented at the Leveson Inquiry. We have to send the message to members of parliament and to the government that we care about this and that we will be angry if, by some fix or fudge, the editors and proprietors are given yet another last chance. And we have to stick at this, at the moments when it matters, for as long as it takes.

What can you do?

As a first step, you can support Hacked Off, which is helping coordinate the campaign for change. Hacked Off began life in the spring of 2011 when Martin Moore, director of the Media Standards Trust, and the author of this book, Brian Cathcart, professor of journalism at Kingston

University London, were calling for a public inquiry into hacking. It rallied support from thousands of people, among them journalists, academics, victims of press abuse, lawyers and MPs and peers of all parties. In the days after the *Guardian*'s revelations about Milly Dowler, Hacked Off went, with the Dowler family, to see all of the party leaders to urge them to order the kind of public inquiry that could make a difference. It was a time when many argued that such an inquiry was impossible while police investigations were under way, but we said no, it could be done. We also argued strongly that, because of the history of press abuses, the inquiry should extend beyond voicemail hacking to the culture, ethics and practices of the press. And we said it should cover relations between the press and both politicians and the police. Our arguments were accepted and the inquiry was set up immediately, with a broad remit and with all-party support. The Prime Minister acknowledged our role when he made the announcement.

Over the nine months of public hearings we have remained close to the victims and their lawyers, where necessary helping them to participate in the process and tell their stories. We have reported the inquiry online – in a fashion markedly different from, and more thorough than, most of the national papers. We have commented on the evidence. We have made submissions not only to the Leveson Inquiry but also to a number of other relevant bodies. And we have highlighted instances of continuing press abuse. On occasion, notably over its skimpy treatment of Motorman, we have criticized the inquiry. Although we have had support from celebrities such as Steve Coogan and Hugh Grant – and we are grateful for it – we are not merely a mouthpiece for the famous. (We also reject the notion that fame automatically robs people of their right to fair treatment by the press.) Thousands of ordinary people follow the activities of Hacked Off because they care about the state of journalism and of the press, and because they are angry about press abuses. We believe strongly that millions of people care about what has gone wrong in our national press and that they want something better, and we are working hard to send that message to parliament and to the government, and to put the arguments to MPs and ministers. For example, every MP is receiving a copy of this book – free.

We need your active and sustained support.

- Please go online (WWW.hackinginquiry.org) and make contact with us. Register your email address so that we can keep you informed about what we are doing.
- Please follow us on Twitter or Facebook.
- Please write to your MP to tell him or her how you feel about this issue. This is not a waste of time, especially if it is your own letter and not a pro forma.
- Please write to the editors of the newspapers you read and let them know your feelings.
- Please encourage any relevant clubs, societies or other organizations to which you belong to engage with Hacked Off, because we want to show how much Britain's 'big society' cares about this. If we can, we will help find a speaker for a meeting or public event.
- Please persuade other people to do the same things, and also to buy this book and spread the word.

- Please go to our website and make a donation. We may eventually receive royalties from this book but the price is low and they will never add up to very much. So we need funds to support our activities. To date a number of donors – both individuals and institutions – have kept us going, along with our online donations, but our adversaries are multimillion-pound corporations and we need more. Please give as much as you can.

- Finally, please stay with this. If we allow the press or the politicians to believe that we are losing interest, the battle is probably lost. That has always happened in the past. Let us make it different this time.

And remember: no more last chances, no delays, no fixes and no fudges. We want real change this time.

Notes

1. http://inforrm.wordpress.com/2012/06/09/australian-media-you-wouldnt-read-about-it-everything-you-wanted-to-know-about-media-accountability-and-the-finkelstein-inquiry-matthew-ricketson/

2. http://www.ippr.org/press-releases/111/9185/more-than-three-quarters-of-public-want-strict-regulation-of-the-press-

3. http://www.guardian.co.uk/media/interactive/2012/jan/23/phone-hacking-surrey-police-milly-dowler

4. http://www.independent.co.uk/news/uk/crime/full-text-of-clive-goodmans-letter-to-news-international-2338523.html

5. http://www.publications.parliament.uk/pa/cm201012/cmselect/cmcumeds/903/903we64.htm

6. http://www.publications.parliament.uk/pa/cm201012/cmselect/cmcumeds/903/90310.htm

7. http://www.bjr.org.uk/current

8. http://www.youtube.com/watch?v=wtcq8RDDPFU

9. http://www.itv.com/news/2012-03-28/newspaper-payments-for-potentially-illegal-information-revealed/

10. http://www.levesoninquiry.org.uk/wp-content/uploads/2012/01/Witness-Statement-of-Liz-Hartley.pdf

11. http://www.levesoninquiry.org.uk/wp-content/uploads/2011/11/Operation-Motorman-and-ANL-10-July-2012.pdf

12. http://www.guardian.co.uk/media/2011/mar/11/jonathan-rees-private-investigator-tabloid

13. http://www.guardian.co.uk/commentisfree/2007/sep/10/comment.pressandpublishing

14. http://www.guardian.co.uk/media/greenslade/2011/jan/13/express-newspapers-medialaw

15. http://www.guardian.co.uk/commentisfree/2011/jul/08/press-regulation-press-complaints-commission

16. http://hansard.millbanksystems.com/commons/1990/jun/21/calcutt-report

17. http://www.official-documents.gov.uk/document/cm21/2135/2135.pdf

18. http://mediastandardstrust.org/wp-content/uploads/downloads/2012/06/MST-A-Free-and-Accountable-Media-21-06-12.pdf

19. http://www.publications.parliament.uk/pa/cm200910/cmselect/cmcumeds/362/362ii.pdf

20. http://www.levesoninquiry.org.uk/wp-content/uploads/2012/06/Submission-by-MediaWise1.pdf

21. http://www.levesoninquiry.org.uk/wp-content/uploads/2011/11/Transcript-of-Morning-Hearing-22-November-20111.pdf

22. http://www.levesoninquiry.org.uk/wp-content/uploads/2011/11/Witness-Statement-of-Charlotte-Church.pdf

23. http://www.levesoninquiry.org.uk/wp-content/uploads/2011/11/Transcript-of-Morning-Hearing-24-November-2011.pdf

24. http://www.itv.com/news/2012-03-28/newspaper-payments-for-potentially-illegal-information-revealed/

25. http://www.levesoninquiry.org.uk/wp-content/uploads/2012/01/Transcript-of-Morning-Hearing-11-January-2012.pdf

26. http://www.levesoninquiry.org.uk/wp-content/uploads/2012/02/Second-Witness-Statement-of-DAC-Sue-Akers.pdf

27. http://www.levesoninquiry.org.uk/wp-content/uploads/2012/01/Transcript-of-Morning-Hearing-12-January-2012.pdf

28. http://www.newstatesman.com/blogs/steven-baxter/2012/01/anonymous-sources-public

29. http://www.bbc.co.uk/news/business-18854193

30. http://www.levesoninquiry.org.uk/wp-content/uploads/2012/07/Transcript-of-Morning-Hearing-9-July-2012.txt

31. http://hackinginquiry.org/news/huntblack-plan-fails-the-prime-minister's-dowlermccann-test/

32. http://www.levesoninquiry.org.uk/wp-content/uploads/2012/06/Joint-Submission-by-Core-Participant-Victims1.pdf

33. http://www.bjr.org.uk/data/2012/no2_barnett

34. http://www.guardian.co.uk/media/2012/jul/15/leveson-wears-thin-press-money-matters

35. http://www.guardian.co.uk/media/2011/oct/19/lord-chief-justice-press-regulation?newsfeed=true

Owners and Editors of National Newspapers Since 2000

Publication	Owner or dominant shareholder	Editor
The Times	Rupert Murdoch 1981–	Peter Stothard 1992–2002 Robert Thomson 2002–7 James Harding 2007–
Sunday Times	Rupert Murdoch 1981–	John Witherow 1994–
Sun	Rupert Murdoch 1969–	David Yelland 1998–2003 Rebekah Wade 2003–9 Dominic Mohan 2009–
News of the World	Rupert Murdoch 1969–2011	Rebekah Wade 2000–2003 Andy Coulson 2003–7 Colin Myler 2007–11
Sun on Sunday	Rupert Murdoch 2011–	Dominic Mohan 2012–
Daily Mirror	Trinity Mirror plc 1999–	Piers Morgan 1995–2004 Richard Wallace 2004–12 Lloyd Embley 2012–
Sunday Mirror	Trinity Mirror plc 1999–	Colin Myler 1998–2001 Tina Weaver 2001–12 Lloyd Embley 2012–
People	Trinity Mirror plc 1999–	Neil Wallis 1998–2003 Mark Thomas 2003–8 Lloyd Embley 2008–12 James Scott 2012–

Daily Mail	Lord Rothermere 1998– (The paper has been owned by the Harmsworth family since 1896)	Paul Dacre 1992–
Mail on Sunday	Lord Rothermere 1998–	Peter Wright 1998–2012 Geordie Greig 2012–
Daily Express	Richard Desmond 2000–	Rosie Boycott 1998–2001 Chris Williams 2001–3 Peter Hill 2003–11 Hugh Whittow 2011–
Sunday Express	Richard Desmond 2000–	Michael Pilgrim 1999–2001 Martin Townsend 2001–
Daily Star	Richard Desmond 2000–	Peter Hill 1998–2003 Dawn Neesom 2003–
Daily Star Sunday	Richard Desmond 2002–	Hugh Whittow 2002–3 Gareth Morgan 2003–
Daily Telegraph	Conrad, Lord Black 1986–2004 Sir David & Sir Frederick Barclay 2004–	Charles Moore 1995–2003 Martin Newland 2003–5 John Bryant 2005–6 William Lewis 2006–9 Tony Gallagher 2009–
Sunday Telegraph	Conrad, Lord Black 1986–2004 Sir David & Sir Frederick Barclay 2004–	Dominic Lawson 1995–2005 Sarah Sands 2005–6 Patience Wheatcroft 2006–7 Ian MacGregor 2007–
Guardian	Scott Trust 1936–	Alan Rusbridger 1995–

Observer	Scott Trust 1936–	Roger Alton 1998–2007 John Mulholland 2008–
Independent	Sir Tony O'Reilly, Gavin O'Reilly 1998–2010 Lebedev family 2010–	Simon Kelner 1998–2008 Roger Alton 2008–10 Simon Kelner 2010–11 Chris Blackhurst 2011–
Independent on Sunday	Sir Tony O'Reilly, Gavin O'Reilly 1998–2010 Lebedev family 2010–	Janet Street–Porter 1999–2002 Tristan Davies 2002–8 John Mullin 2008–
i	Lebedev family 2010–	Simon Kelner 2010–11 Stefano Hatfield 2011–
Financial Times	Pearson plc 1957–	Richard Lambert 1991–2001 Andrew Gowers 2001–5 Lionel Barber 2005–